UNDERSTANDING
The New Testament

H.L. Ellison

1 Peter   2 Peter

1 John   2 John   3 John

Jude

Revelation

A BIBLE STUDY BOOK

Published in Great Britain by
Scripture Union
47 Marylebone Lane, London W1 6AX

© 1969 Scripture Union
First published 1969

Republished in Daily Bible Commentary 1974
Reprinted 1977
First published in this edition 1978

ISBN 0 85421 606 5

Printed and bound in Great Britain by
McCorquodale (Newton) Ltd, Newton-le-Willows

INTRODUCTION

Since their introduction, Scripture Union Bible Study Books have enjoyed wide popularity both in their original paperback and more recently as the hardback Daily Bible Commentary. The continued demand has led to their production in this new format. They are unique in that they can be used both as a daily Bible reading aid and as a complete commentary on the New Testament.

A Daily Bible Reading Aid

Each volume is divided into sections of an appropriate length for daily use. Normally each volume provides material for one quarter's use, the exceptions being Mark (two months) and 1 and 2 Corinthians and Galatians (four months). Sections have not been dated but where it has been felt appropriate that two be read together in order to complete the book within a quarter they are marked with an asterisk.

A complete commentary of the New Testament

Every major passage is expounded with devotional warmth, clear explanations and relevance to daily life. Most commentaries follow the rather artificial verse divisions, but here the writers have been commissioned to divide the material according to the best exegetical pattern. They thus follow natural units which allow the comments to follow more closely the flow of the original writers thought.

Writers have generally based their comments on the R.S.V. and readers will probably find this is the most suitable translation to use, although the comments will be found equally helpful with any other version.

1 and 2 Peter, Jude

1 Peter was written to the scattered Christians of northern and western Asia Minor, an area which was mainly outside the sphere of Paul's missionary work. Various references make it clear that the majority of the intended readers were Gentiles. Silvanus (5.12), i.e. Silas, Paul's companion on his second missionary journey, may have interested Peter in the area. The excellent Greek is probably due to Silvanus having acted as scribe. The letter was probably written from Rome (5.13), possibly after the beginning of Nero's persecution.

The language of *2 Peter* is very different, but this can be explained by Peter's using a different scribe, for there is no marked difference in thought. The recipients of the letter are not named, but since this letter was perhaps the last book to be accepted into the Canon, it was probably not written to an influential church. The chief reason why many reject the Petrine authorship is the way he speaks of Paul's letters (3.15 f.), but the argument is hardly valid. The same may be said of the use of *Jude*, the message of which Peter may have wished to make better known.

Jude was almost certainly written by our Lord's brother of that name. The fact that most of the letter was taken up by Peter into his second letter suggests that it was originally addressed to a limited circle. It is concerned with those who were both false teachers and false livers, as were so many who were influenced by early Gnosticism, cf. Rev. 2,3.

1 Peter 1.1-9   The Preciousness of Faith

With the doubtful exception of Gal. 6.16, the name Israel is not applied to the Church in the N.T., but the various descriptions of it are. Peter uses here and in 2.11 three such terms. 'Dispersion' (1) was the regular term for the Jew living outside Palestine; the Christian's homeland is heaven. 'Exiles' (also in 2.11, cf. 1.17), better, sojourners, is rendered excellently 'who lodge for a while' by the NEB. The stress is on the short while we are here. Then there is 'aliens' in 2.11. The stress is that the Christian, not being a citizen of this world, cf. Phil. 3.20, has no rights here. They are Christians by a threefold act of the Trinity (though the word is not used):

chosen by the Father, made holy by the Spirit, consecrated by the blood of the Son (see NEB).

'Grace and peace' (2): the former includes the experience of God's covenant love, the latter the opening of God's treasure chamber. This fact leads to a benediction. 'Blessed' (3) virtually means that we accept this in gratitude on bended knees. Central is Jesus' resurrection. His new life has started a new life in us which expects to reach Him in heaven. He is our inheritance which we shall obtain at His coming. Because it is a person, not a thing, it is 'imperishable' (4), etc. While it is there secure for us in heaven, we are kept for Him down here, because 'the power from without corresponds to the faith within' (Hort).

We can never be sure of anything until it has been tested—'temptations' (6, AV[KJV]) had this meaning earlier—and so we must pass through testings or 'trials' (6), which can be very painful. Paul assures us we shall never be overtested (1 Cor. **10**.13), and the outcome is that we know our faith is not merely something we have produced, but it has been given us by God. Victory in trial shows that the faith came from God, so it is 'precious' (7), and can be the cause of praise and glory. Peter was doubtless thinking of Christ's words to Thomas (John **20**.29), when he wrote 'without having seen Him' (8). The rendering of 'the salvation of your souls' (9) can be misleading. For the Bible the soul is the whole of a man including his body.

Thought: *Salvation is complete!*

1 Peter 1.10-12   The Faith of the Prophets

Peter's readers might legitimately have asked why *their* faith should be so specially important. Where Paul referred to Abraham and *Hebrews* to a long line of the faithful, Peter turned to the prophets. In contrast to the predominant modern view, which sees them as little more than clear-sighted interpreters of their own time, he followed the Rabbinic maxim, 'No prophet ever prophesied except for the days of the Messiah.' This did not mean that they did not prophesy for their own time—stupidity was not one of the Rabbinic faults—but that they saw their own time in the light of the day of the Lord. Peter said that they were so convinced that they were giving God's message, that they committed themselves to it before they knew to whom it applied or when it would come to fulfilment.

To be noted is that they showed deeper interest in the salvation (10) than in the time (11). The term 'the Spirit of Christ' is found

4

again in Rom. **8**.9. Here it means that they were so possessed by the Spirit of the Messiah that they were able to see coming suffering and glory with His eyes.

In addition, however, they saw that they were foretelling the salvation of those to whom Peter was writing, i.e. the Church. It has often been suggested that the prophets could not discern the interval between the first and second comings of Christ, just as when a man viewing two parallel ranges of mountains from a distance cannot know the deep valley that separates them. With all the truth in this view it is inadequate. Throughout the O.T. God is praised as Saviour. But there is always an element of inadequacy in it and hence a looking to the future. This is succinctly summed up in Heb. **11**.39 f. Not only has Christ entered into His glory (Luke **24**.26), but we share in it, e.g. Gal. **2**.20; Col. **3**.1–4. It is not merely that we shall experience 'the powers of the world to come', but we have tasted them already (Heb. **6**.5). Eternity is projected into time, the glory of Christ may be seen before His return in the Church, and therefore the salvation which the prophets hoped for has become a reality through our faith.

1 Peter 1.13-21   The Life of Faith

So wonderful is our salvation that 'angels stoop down to look' (12), so Peter turns to our responsibility. His readers were to 'pull themselves together'. The growing hostility to the Christians which came to a climax in the Neronian persecution in Rome, doubtless copied in the provinces, evidently made them feel a little sorry for themselves. It is not clear whether we are to take 'be sober' literally or as 'perfectly self-controlled' (NEB); Eph. **5**.18 is sufficient evidence that undue drinking did take place. They were to set their hope 'fully': there is always the temptation to hope that there may be some private relaxation. Selwyn is probably correct with 'the blessing that is being conferred on you in the Lord's appearing.'

Since their hope was set on the future, they had to be 'obedient' (14). The combination of 'passions' and 'ignorance' strongly suggests Gentile readers. Since they were children, they should show the character of the Father (15-17). Note that v. 16, just like Lev. **19**.2, can just as well be rendered 'You will be holy . . .' Sanctification, the making holy, is the work of the Holy Spirit who separates those for God—the meaning of holy—who are willing to be separated. 'Stand in awe' (NEB), or conduct yourselves 'reverently' (Selwyn), is better than 'fear' (17). 'Your exile': cf. note on **1**.1.

'You were ransomed' (18): to ransom or redeem belongs to the standard language of salvation in the O.T. The question to whom the price is paid is never raised; what is of importance is that God frees the slave. It is Mark **10.**45 that makes clear that a price has to be paid, though even here no recipient is suggested. The 'futile ways' (18) are probably idolatry. Many are tempted to think of God like an earthly ruler, adapting his policy to circumstances. Even if the AV(KJV) of 2 Sam. **14.**14 were correct (see RSV), it would not be a revelation of God's way of working, but the crafty argument of Joab and the woman. The cross is an essential part of God's purpose antedating the creation (20). Neither the fall of Satan nor of man took God by surprise. 'At the end of the times' (20), or ages; we are in the final age already, though only those who know Christ can enjoy the powers of the coming age.

Thought: We must not tarnish God's triumph.

1 Peter 1.22—2.3   The Soil for Love

Great though faith is, it takes second place to love. Peter remembered that his passionate devotion to his Master brought him a stinging rebuke (Matt. **16.**23) and did not keep him from denying Him. Christian love is a fruit of the Spirit, borne by the 'purified soul' (22). The NEB gets the sense '. . . you have purified your souls until you feel sincere affection.' The evil things mentioned in **2.**1 are weeds which effectively smother the growth of love. Some of those who complain of lack of love may find the clue to their trouble here. It may seem strange, but love is not one of those quiet virtues that grows best when least observed; the more we actually love, the more we shall be able to. Furthermore it is a long-term virtue. Many think that life is so short that they dare not give themselves unrestrainedly in love. We have been reborn for eternity, and love is one of the few things we can carry with us.

'Pure spiritual milk' (2): it is very doubtful whether Peter is making the distinction found in Heb. **5.**12–14; 1 Cor. **3.**1 f., where milk represents the simpler and more fundamental facts of the gospel. For the babe to remain in good health and grow, he needs food regularly. The adult may be able to fast or go on iron rations for days at a time, but not the baby. That is why regular habits of Bible study and prayer are so important for the new convert. 'Pure' (2): unadulterated. For us adulteration means the addition of some noxious substance, but here any addition is implied. The uninterested, blinded outsider may need some bait to get him to listen. For the baby, born by the work of the Holy Spirit, such things are unnecessary. We must not water down our teaching, or add the sugar of sentimentality. On the other hand we must not offer that dehydration of the Word, which we call theology.

Thought: Be sure to speak a good word for your Lord.

1 Peter 2.4-10   The Honour of Christ's People

There is a complete change of subject. In a theological treatise this would be strange, but not in a letter. There are many examples of this in Paul's writings. Up to this point Peter has been thinking of his readers as individuals, but now of them as linked together in the Church. A comparison of vs. 6–8 with Rom. **9.**33; Acts **4.**11; Mark **12.**10 f., will show that the N.T. wove together Isa. **8.**10–15; **28.**15f.; Psa. **118.**19–23, and applied them to Christ. We know from Qumran that such linking of Scripture was already common there.

'That living stone' (4): the Greek word implies not a rock, as in Matt. **16.**18, but one that has been shaped, cf. Heb. **2.**10,18; **5.**9, etc. It is not merely to the eternal Son of God that we come, but to Jesus, the God-man. If He was shaped, so are we, so that all together we may form a spiritual temple, cf. 1 Cor. **3.**16 f.; 2 Cor. **6.**16–18; Eph. **2.**19–22. In the notes on Rev. **21.**22. there are comments on a temple as that which separates God from man; here the temple enables God to live among men, even though they reject Him. Not the church building, but the company of faithful Christians is the house of God.

Because the temple is built with living stones, they are simultaneously the priests that minister in it. The 'spiritual sacrifices' (5) are not that of Rom. **12.**1, which is individual. These refer to the work of the local church as an organism. They include the worship of the church, but surely also all those activities that reveal the character of God to men. The very vagueness of Peter's language indicates that he was not thinking of something limited and definite.

The quotations that follow do not link logically with v.5, but with Peter's thought as a whole. 'He is precious' (7); it is doubtful whether this is the meaning. We should probably take it as 'To you who believe He is honour', i.e. belief ensures honour to those who believe. The NEB rendering, 'The great worth of which it speaks is for you', expresses this thought. The honour is the spiritual reality of the promise made to Israel (Exod. **19.**5 f.). 'A royal priesthood' in the light of the O.T. and Rev. **1.**6 (see notes) probably means a priesthood in the service of the King, i.e. God. 'A holy nation': both in Hebrew and Greek, the word for nation is that used for the nations in general, the Gentiles; it is holiness that makes Israel and the Church different.

1 Peter 2.11-17   Caesar and God

Once again the subject changes. Peter urges his readers to behave as 'aliens' and sojourners (see note on **1.**1) should, cf. Phil. **3.**17-21. As aliens in this world there is no compulsion for them to live as worldlings. The world will malign them (12)—the foreigner is always suspect—but on the day of judgement ('visitation') it will acknowledge the truth before God; in Josh. **7.**19 the phrase is used in the sense of 'tell the truth'.

For vs. 13, 14, cf. Rom. **13.**1-7. The Christian is a free man (16), a citizen of heaven (Phil. **3.**20), and yet he is to accept the world-order around him. That is because it is based on law, and the apostles knew that bad law is better than lawlessness and chaos. They would not have regarded the totalitarian tendency to 'legalize' the wrongs it has committed as the rule of law. The difference is that under law one knows what is prohibited, under chaos one is at the mercy of those in power at the moment. The quiet bearing of injustice under the guise of law is always harder than plotting the overthrow of the unjust, but it is also always more effective in the long run.

Later portions of the letter make it clear that Peter knew that his readers might and would suffer for their loyalty to God, e.g. **3.**13-17; **4.**1, 12-16, but that did not alter the principle. If Christ suffered unjustly, so can we. When Jesus said, 'Give to Caesar the things that are Caesar's, and to God the things that are God's' (Mark **12.**17), we often overlook that what is Caesar's has been given him by God. To most believers comes the moment when they have to say to those in authority in the home, the church, the State, 'Here I take my stand; I can do nothing else, so help me God.' When this happens there is suffering and blessing. Unfortunately most of us take our stand on ground of our choosing, not Christ's; then there is strife and division, not blessing. So often difficulties arise because we do not honour *all* men (17); we regard them as potential salvation fodder, but no more.

Thought: God rules in the affairs of men.

Slavery was legal, and God had given His qualified recognition of it by legislating about it. So slaves—not 'servants' (18)—provided perhaps the extremest and most painful example of being subject to human institutions (13). Though little slavery remains in the world today there is much subordination; economic, social, traditional. Sometimes it is good and right, sometimes abhorrent. Whenever the attempt to throw it off is made we discover that where there is no inner freedom, outward freedom leads only to new slavery. In addition, men are discovering that where they are not willing to serve, they will not be served in the hour of need.

It was Christ who came not to be served but to serve (Mark 10.45), so He is the pattern for those who serve. If the slave is willing to serve for Christ's sake, as his God-given vocation, then the sting of slavery has gone. He is also the example for those who suffer injustice and abuse from those who abuse their positions (21–23). Few Christians grasp what a privilege it is (painful, of course) to be allowed to share the injustice Christ suffered.

The RSV margin is correct in v. 24, cf. NEB. Peter here assumes, but does not stress, the death of Christ; it is that which went before and prepared for that death that occupies him. Jesus was not suddenly identified with our sins when the nails were driven into His hands and feet. All that had gone before was part of His self-identification with our sins. He carried them 'to the tree', the burden becoming heavier as He went. While to render John the Baptist's words, 'Behold, the Lamb of God, who takes away the sin of the world' (John 1.29), is to draw out their full meaning, literally he said, 'Who carries the sin of the world'.

Concepts like these throw light on Paul's remarkable statement in Col. 1.24. We cannot share in Christ's atoning work, except to profit from it, but we can share in His sufferings. When we think of His life, we are apt to think of Him living under Jewish law, the law of God, even if distorted by Pharisaic reasoning. We forget that Palestine was under Roman colonial law as well, with all its brutality and frequent arbitrariness.

Thought: Christ is the special Patron of those who serve.

Questions for further study and discussion on 1 Peter chs. 1,2

1. What does the phrase 'exiles (sojourners) of the Dispersion' (1.1) suggest concerning the Christian's proper attitude to the

world and the State? (See **1.**17; **2.**11–17, and collect other N.T. references, e.g. Phil. **3.**20; Rom. **12,13.**)

2. Starting from **2.**4,5, discuss the Christian's responsibility in and to the Church.
3. How can **2.**18–20 be applied to modern conditions of employment, with (a) a Christian, and (b) a non-Christian, employer?
4. In what ways do both this passage and 1 John **3** link together the themes of sinful behaviour and brotherly love?

1 Peter 3.1-7   Marriage

From slavery, and by implication, all similar forms of subjection, Peter passes to marriage. He uses the same word, 'submissive', for the wife as for the slave (**2.**18) and the younger church member (**5.**5). The NEB is correct in the first two cases in rendering 'accept the authority', and this would have been best in the third as well. God has ordered His creation on the basis of authority and subordination, and Peter is calling on us to respect God's order. Relative subordination in this world disappears in a common subordination to Christ, before whom we all stand on the same footing. The difficulty felt in Peter's teaching by many today would in great measure vanish, if we took 'honour all men' (**2.**17) seriously. Not 'obey', but 'honour' is the difficult word for many in the marriage promise.

Some of his readers were women married to unbelievers, Jewish or pagan (1). Peter says it is their lives rather than their words that may win their husbands. Both Paul, in 1 Tim. **2.**9f., and Peter concentrate on the same point. The 'hair-do', the ornaments and the striking dresses, where they are not intended to put the neighbours' noses out of joint, are to boost the woman's ego. In contrast to modern concepts the Church's wedding robe in Rev. **19.**8 (see note) is for the glory of the Bridegroom. The women Peter describes are dressing for themselves, not their husbands. Phillips may be correct in paraphrasing, 'do not give way to hysterical fears' (6). Many marriages are wrecked by deep-rooted fears. If a woman simply trusts her marriage, children and husband to God and does not think she must fight to preserve it, she will find fear vanishing.

When he turns to the husbands, Peter does not rise to the heights of Eph. **5.**25, but he should be understood in the same way. 'With understanding' (NEB) is far superior to 'considerately' (7). It is true of us all that 'we are fearfully and wonderfully made', but this is truer of the woman than of the man. By the time a young husband has really come to understand his wife—and great consideration is needed for this—he will find that she will probably want to accept his authority. If he does not remember that she is his equal spiritually, he will diminish his own spiritual standing and not be able to pray properly (7).

1 Peter 3.8-12   Mutual Submission

Just as in Eph. 5.21,22, Peter sees marriage as only a special case of general relationships. While 'unity of spirit' (8) is created by the Holy Spirit, it is far more than the one Spirit living in us all. If I do not try to find out what my fellow Christian is thinking, I cannot be one with him. If I do not discover what he is feeling, I cannot suffer with him, the meaning of 'sympathy'. 'A tender heart', literally, 'with healthy intestines'; it means a well-balanced reaction to the situation of those I meet. I must neither be carried away by my feelings, nor deal with him purely intellectually. 'The humble mind' enables me to show him the honour that is his by right (2.17) and by the fact that, like me, he is God's child. Should anyone object that too high a standard is being demanded, Peter quotes Christ's own words (Matt. 5.39,44). The 'blessing' we obtain is found in Matt. 5.45. Sometimes we feel that someone deserves an 'ear-ful' of what he is really like ('reviling') or a dose of his own medicine ('return evil'); we should remember Christ's words then (Matt. 5.45,48).

Peter develops the thought of the blessing by quoting Psa. 34.12–16. The two features stressed are a check on one's words, i.e. not reviling, and turning from evil. The blessing is life, good days, and prayers that are heard. When we hear complaints about discord in the local church, lack of love, and unkind actions and judgements, we should do well to look at the one who complains. Very often his own life is an epitome of the things he complains about. We may give him the benefit of the doubt and say he did not begin the trouble, but he has seen to it that the troubles continue.

Thought: If we want others to be different let us set them an example.

1 Peter 3.13-22   Christ's Triumph

It might be argued that self-assertion is necessary in this evil world. 'God cares for those who care for themselves' is a frequently met maxim. Peter makes no secret of the probability that they will have to suffer for righteousness' sake. Apparent defeat will be merely

11

the way to victory. It should be noted, however, that we are far more likely to suffer, if we are zealous for other people to do right, than if the zeal is applied to our own lives (13).

Christ's death combined with His resurrection represents God's greatest triumph (18). In the natural realm ('in the flesh') He was put to death; in the spiritual realm He was made alive—His bodily resurrection is the sequel to, and the consequence of, this, cf. Acts 2.24. In the course of which ('in which') He made proclamation of His triumph ('preached') to the angels ('spirits'; the word is not used of dead men) imprisoned in the days of Noah, cf. Jude 6. They had done their very best to destroy the world (Gen. 6.1–8), and had apparently succeeded, for all but eight persons were over-whelmed by the Flood. To them, and presumably to any other fallen angels awaiting their final judgement, came the knowledge that their utmost efforts had been defeated. The idea that Christ was proclaiming His salvation to those overwhelmed by the Flood does not seem to play any part here, the more so as they were merely a special case of a common problem (see notes on Rev. 20.11–15).

The transference of thought to Christian baptism (21) is an easy one, but there is much to be said for the theory that this letter represents an expansion of a baptismal sermon. Baptism springs from Christ's triumph, cf. Rom 6.3 f. The Ark was the symbol of God's triumph and saving power in the midst of corruption, and so is baptism. 'Not as a removal of dirt from the body' (21): the 'baptisms' of Qumran were largely an extension of the ceremonial washings of the Temple and of the Pharisees (Mark 7.3 f.) intended to remove physical defilement. Baptism so cleanses the inner man, or represents his cleansing, that 'with a good conscience we can appeal to God' or 'make a pledge to Him for a new life'. The RSV 'an appeal to God for a clear conscience' is improbable, and the other rendering should have appeared at least in the margin.

Thought: The eye of faith sees the Ark, not the flood-waters.

1 Peter 4.1-11   Life in the Last Days

Not the fear of death, but of dying, dogs the feet of very many Christians. Christ's sufferings (1) are His death; so the Christian's death will mean triumph, i.e. 'ceasing from sin'. But in the measure in which he shares Christ's sufferings he will cease sinning, for he places himself by so doing under 'the will of God' (2).

The Jew was notorious among the Gentiles for his refusal to share their meals and junketings, so vs. 3,4 are very strong evidence that the bulk of Peter's readers were Gentiles. It is likely that the AV (KJV) 'abominable idolatries' (3) is preferable to 'lawless idolatry'. We are not called on to sit in judgement on the immorality around us; we have simply to proclaim that there will be a Divine judgement. We do not escape this judgement by death. Though the Christian dead (6) received the common judgement of the flesh, i.e. death, they will live. So for the others there will be the second death (Rev. · 20.14).

'Keep sane' (7): 'Keep your heads' (Selwyn). The final failure of man's devices, of which there is so much in *Revelation*, should find the believer untroubled and prayerful. It is particularly in a time of chaos that the basic virtues find their place. Love can be very difficult when all around men are losing their heads. 'Love covers a multitude of sins' (8): this may well be a saying of Christ's. Its meaning is not clear, for it means more than that love veils the sin of others, cf. 1 Cor. 13.7. Certainly where a person is outstandingly known for love, most people are likely to overlook shortcomings that might otherwise be glaring. Even more, true love can turn others to the source of love, so that they may see Him 'covering' their sins by His blood. 'Hospitality' (9); where church meetings were in private houses, and where there was a tendency to move round so as not to draw undue attention to any one meeting place, hospitality in the widest sense could be a heavy burden. 'A gift' (10) can have a wide range of meaning. The one-sidedness of modern church thought is shown by the exaltation of speaking (11), whereas every form of 'service', because given by Christ, ranks equal with it in the right place.

Thought: God gives the strength to use the gifts He has given.

1 Peter 4.12-19   God's Judgement

Judgement begins 'with the household of God' (17). One of the less considered tensions in Christian theology is that between justification and judgement. This judgement may be experienced in three ways. The tension of Rom. 7.24 f. may be intensified by earlier evil living, especially if it was in defiance of the known will of God. Then there is suffering for the failure of the present, e.g. 1 Cor. 11.29–32 and the warnings to the Seven Churches (Rev. 2,3). Thirdly, there are certain things against which we are specially warned, e.g. Mark 9.42 (does a Christian never do this?); Heb. 4.1; 10.26–31. The clue is probably given by 1 Cor. 11.31.

Here Peter is considering the suffering of Christians as members of the Church, rather than as individuals. Because the Church has fallen short and falls short, its innocent members must suffer together with the guilty. Innocent? All too often wrongdoing in the local church has been possible because of the laxity of standards. Neither now nor before the judgement seat of Christ can the Lord be indifferent to ungodly living and low standards (2 Cor. 5.10).

If we suffer through no fault of ours, we should rejoice that the judgements of God are doing their work and that we are permitted to share in the sufferings of Christ (13, Col. 1.24). We must, however, be careful. Experience suggests that when we are most wronged, we have by omissions or commissions often helped to create the situation in which we were wronged. God is not interested in legal technicalities.

'The spirit of glory and of God' (14): here glory, literally, the glory, is the equivalent of the Shekinah, or abiding presence of God, i.e. Jesus Christ, cf. John 1.14. So the phrase means the Spirit of Christ in all His glory and of God. 'Mischief-maker' (15): the Greek word in this form occurs only twice, and its meaning is far from certain. Phillips takes it as 'spy', the NEB as 'infringing the rights of others'; the more usual interpretation is 'busybody'. In any case it means putting your nose in where it does not belong. We are slow to learn that where God wants us to intervene in another's life He will give us the knowledge to let us do it with proper effect.

Thought: God never calls black white!

1 Peter 5.1-5
The Elders

Acts shows us clearly enough Peter as the leader of the Twelve, and equally clearly he never forgot the especial charge laid on him to be a shepherd of God's people (John 21.15–17). This will have been his motive in writing the letter, for there is no evidence that he had ever worked in the area to which it is addressed. So he has a special word of exhortation for the elders in the churches to which his letter was sent. He avoids the word shepherd with reference to himself, except by implication, when he calls Christ 'the chief Shepherd' (4), because in the figurative language of the O.T. the shepherd is the king. It is, however, unfortunate that it has been forgotten that true elders are vice-regents. So important are they that Peter claims no authority over them but simply calls himself a 'fellow elder' (1). Yet he had a claim to be heard. He had witnessed the sufferings of

Christ and had seen the Transfiguration—'the glory that is to be revealed' (2 Pet. **1.**16–18).

There are three sets of contrasts: 'constraint', 'shameful gain', 'domineering'—'willingly', 'eagerly', 'examples'; in each case there is a logical and spiritual link. The 'constraint' today comes very often from the failure of the church to realize that the very real spiritual gifts a young man may have do not necessarily qualify him as an elder and pastor. It comes, too, from those who should be pastors, but do not wish to accept the responsibility. The 'crown' is more specifically the victor's crown in the games, cf. 1 Cor. **9.**25 and NEB 'garland'.

The principle of authority applies in the church as everywhere else (5), see notes on **3.**1. Many of our difficulties today come from the elders assuming that because they have authority they have knowledge, and from a younger generation believing that their far more extensive education implies spiritual maturity. Both sides need 'humility' (5). We tend not to take John 7.15,16 sufficiently seriously. Arguing from what we think Jesus should have known, we attribute His authority as a teacher to His knowledge, while He claims it comes from His Father.

Question: What will become of my work if God opposes me?

1 Peter 5.6-14 God's Certain Care

'Humble yourselves' (6); Selwyn points out that it is really 'Allow yourselves to be humbled; accept your humiliations.' 'The mighty hand of God', whether it acts directly, or through persons and things around us, brings us down. There are few things so disgusting or, perhaps, ludicrous, as a person looking for opportunities to be humble. Where God does it, it should be a cause of praise, for we know we shall be exalted, when we can stand the testing involved. The AV(KJV) of v. 7 is misleading, and so to some extent the RSV, for there is no inner link of meaning between 'anxieties . . . cares'. NEB expresses it better, 'Cast all your cares on Him, for you are His charge.'

That God has a concern for us comes not merely from our being His children, but from our being involved in the rear-guard action that Satan still wages against Him (8,9). The lion is at its least dangerous, when it roars. The hunting lion can be amazingly quiet; the roaring (Amos **3.**4) comes when the prey has been secured. So the picture is of a lion trying to do by bluff and intimidation, what it cannot do by stealth and strength. For the idea behind 'the God

15

of all grace' (10) see Phil. **4.19.** Peter does not minimize the power of persecution—after all he had collapsed at the jeers of a servant-girl—but he promises that even if we are shaken by it, God will 'restore' (make good what has gone wrong), 'establish' (set us more firmly on our true foundation), and 'strengthen' (where weakness has been revealed, provide the strength).

Already Papias, early in the second century, understood 'Babylon' to mean Rome. It is not likely that Babylon in Mesopotamia or the one in Egypt would have been suggested, had not some wished to weaken the tradition linking Peter with Rome. The mention of 'Mark', who is linked both with Peter and Rome, supports the traditional view. 'She who is at Babylon' is, of course, the church there, cf. 2 John 1,13.

Questions for further study and discussion on 1 Peter chs. 3–5

1. How would you rephrase 3.1–7 to meet modern conditions?
2. List the mutual responsibilities and attitudes which are essential to the proper functioning of the marriage relationship.
3. What reasons for joy in suffering persecution does Peter list (4.12–14)? Look up references concerning our Lord's and Peter's attitudes to persecution.
4. What duties and dangers are inherent in shepherding the flock of God, and what are the essential qualifications (5.1–4; Ezek. 34; John 21.15–17)?

2 Peter 1.1-11   Christian Growth

There is little doubt that Simeon Peter (1, NEB) is correct, cf. Acts **15.14.** If his first letter, cf. **3.1,** was 1 Peter, then this will have been written when the Neronian persecution was reaching its height. This is sufficient reason for the lack of details about the recipients. 'Obtained' (1): inadequate; the word means to obtain by lot or Divine decree, i.e. all personal merit is excluded. There is only one true 'faith'; the gifts that follow it are diverse. The only linguistically valid interpretation of 'our God and Saviour Jesus Christ' is that Jesus is being called God, cf. **1.11; 2.20; 3.18;** Tit. **2.13.** For 'grace and peace' (2) see note on 1 Pet. **1.2;** the covenant love and riches of God are constant, but our knowledge of God teaches us to draw on them.

In John **17.3** knowledge and salvation are linked (3). While God may reveal to us individually the implications of salvation (1

John 2.26 f.), yet it is a surer method to give us the promises of Scripture (4), which are always greater than our interpretation of them at any given time. The promises do not deliver us from corruption, but stir us up to claim deliverance. With vs. 5–7, cf. Rom. 5.3–5; Gal. 5.22 f. 'Virtue' (5): it is a pity that the link with v. 3 has not been indicated, where the word is rendered 'excellence'; the quality is something coming from God. 'Knowledge' is not that human quality condemned by Paul in *1 Corinthians*, but a gift from the Holy Spirit giving us true balance in judgement. 'Self-control' (6) without knowledge and balance is likely to become asceticism or fanaticism; similarly 'steadfastness' without self-control is liable to lead to an explosion. 'Godliness', cf. v. 3: piety (NEB) or devotion to God (Phillips) are preferable; it refers to a visible quality in life, our attitude to God expressed in actions. The difference between 'brotherly affection' (7, cf. 1 Pet. 1.22; 3.8) and 'love' is not made clear. The former probably has more of the emotional about it.

The child that stops growing becomes a monstrosity. When a man stops developing mentally he has taken the first step to senility. This is even truer with spiritual growth, the more so as the purpose of our salvation is that we should become like Christ, cf. 2 Cor. 3.18; 1 John 3.2. 'To confirm your call' (10): the necessity to respond to God's call does not end with conversion.

Question: Have you stopped growing?

2 Peter 1.12-18   The Assurance of Christ's Return

At the time he wrote this letter Peter was already an old man as things were then reckoned. It is not likely that he had had a special revelation of his coming death (14); it is more likely that he foresaw that the prediction of John 21.18 would soon come to pass. This letter is referred to in v. 15. They would be able to refer to it at any time.

Clearly the difficulty in the minds of those to whom he was writing was not the resurrection of Christ, but that the One who had lived here in humility could ever conquer the world—the dream of the Church in the days of its dominance, that it would conquer the world for Jesus, had not crossed their mind. Indications of this doubt may be traced here and there in *1 Peter*. If Christ could not keep His own from suffering, how could He triumph? So Peter reminds us that he had seen His Divine 'majesty' (16)—the word is not used of men—break through on the Mount of Transfiguration.

This had been confirmed by the glory which came from the majesty on high and the voice which acknowledged Him (17). In other words, His earthly poverty and humility had been assumed and were not the expression of His real nature, cf. Phil. 2.5–8. Equally then, the humility and poverty of the Church were a cloak hiding its true nature.

Today, also, every effort is being made to show that the N.T. teaching about the Return of Christ is mere myth (16); it is doubtful whether the term 'cleverly devised' would even be granted them. We may differ about the how and when, but the N.T. teaches clearly that the Creator of the world came into His creation (John 1.10 f.) and won or redeemed it for Himself. Whatever the future of the world (see notes on Rev. 21,22), He does not abandon His creation to futility (Rom. 8.18–23), but will achieve His original purpose with it. The world, too, is capable of transformation.

Thought: We are to witness the vindication of Christ as Creator as well as Saviour.

2 Peter 1.19—2.3   The Interpretation of Prophecy

We have today a strong and growing stress on religious experience. In so far as this is Spirit produced, it is valid and not to be despised. But even Peter let his experience on the Mount of Transfiguration step into second place behind the prophetic Scriptures, which for him included the *Pentateuch* and the historical books from *Joshua* to *2 Kings*, apart from *Ruth*. 'We have the prophetic word made more sure' (19): the Greek is ambiguous. It may mean as in the NEB margin, 'In the message of the prophets we have something still more certain'. It is not so important, for Peter does not ask his readers to look away from the prophets but rather 'to pay attention' (19). For 'the morning star' see note on Rev. 22.16.

There are certain points to be remembered about prophecy. The oriental 'lamp' illuminated only the immediate surroundings. Prophecy is not that we should know the details of the future, but that we may understand the future, when it becomes the present. Then no prophecy 'is of any private interpretation'; since prophecy came from the Holy Spirit, it must be interpreted by the Holy Spirit. The Church is far from infallible, but an interpretation rejected by spiritual men after due thought and prayer is not likely to be correct. It also means, however, that since prophecy is a unity because it all comes from the same Spirit, we have no right to take a passage and interpret it in isolation from the rest. Our greatest weakness in Bibli-

18

cal exegesis, and not merely in our interpretation of prophecy, comes from our frequent ignoring of this principle. The prophets 'were impelled by the Holy Spirit' (21, NEB). Peter is not denying the very real personal contribution of the prophet to his message, but that it was in any way something thought out and shaped by him.

Yet 'false prophets' (1) have been, just as there are false teachers. Much in the later prophetic writing is devoted to false prophets; see especially Jer. **23.**9–40. The characteristics of the false teachers are that in one way or another they disown their Master (NEB), they are licentious, and they exploit their hearers. The proportions of these vary from false teacher to false teacher, but they are always present. Peter is not thinking of those who do not claim to be Christians.

2 Peter 2.4-16   False Prophets and Teachers

Peter in this chapter largely reproduces Jude 4–16. The humility which is apparent in both his letters probably made him consider that Jude had expressed himself far better than he could.

The remarkable thing about the false prophets and teachers (1) is that they ignore the long list of warning judgements. 'The angels when they sinned' (4): cf. note on 1 Pet. **3.**19 f. Clearly this does not refer to Satan. 'Cast them into hell', literally into Tartarus; it is a pity that RSV has translated as it has, for hell has taken on the meaning of Gehenna, or the lake of fire (Rev. **19.**20; **20.**14). Tartarus was the lowest abyss of Hades. The Flood and the destruction of Sodom and Gomorrah left an indelible impression on Israel. 'Lot' (7) is mentioned, as is 'Noah' (5), to make quite clear that these catastrophes were not merely natural events. The deliverance of the only righteous people among those destroyed showed God's guiding hand over all. 'Defiling passion' (10): the presence of false teaching shows itself almost invariably in an ascetic depreciation of marriage or in a denial of its bonds. 'Despise authority': those whom Peter condemns either thought they could prophesy by their own impulse or denied the apostolic authority in the Church.

'They are not afraid to revile' (10); for the comment on this verse and the next see that on Jude 8,9; Peter abbreviates here. By their despising God's order they have sunk to the level of animals (12) and will go to their destruction blindly. 'To revel in the daytime' (13): contrast Peter's indignant comment in Acts **2.**15. Work is also part of God's order, not merely a result of the fall (Gen. **2.**15).

19

The NEB gets the sense better, 'While they sit with you at table they are an ugly blot on your company, because they revel in their own deceptions' (13b). 'Eyes full of adultery' (14): they are not merely driven by an insatiable sexual urge; it obtains a special relish in its defiance of the seventh commandment. It is interesting that of the three names given in Jude 11 Peter restricts himself to Balaam. He was a true prophet and feared God. But when the price was big enough he listened to money rather than God. Though he would not prophesy falsely against Israel, he was willing to lead him astray (Num. 31.16).

Thought: The false teacher is worse than the atheist. The latter says there is no God and acts accordingly; the former speaks in His name and defies Him.

2 Peter 2.17-22   False Prophets and Teachers

The tragic description continues. The worst about these men is the way they fail those who put their trust in them. Two pictures are used. 'Waterless springs' (17): for the implications, cf. Job 6.15–20. In the drier Mediterranean lands the traveller plans his route by the known springs and wells. If one of these fails, it means, possibly, death. From these men there comes a sound as of abundance of water springing up, but when one comes to them one finds only wind. Then they are 'mists driven by a storm'. On the wings of the storm-wind, a mist covers the parched land which longs for rain. When the sun comes out again, it is clear that all that has come is a humidity that has merely raised false hopes. The sun is hotter than ever and the mist has vanished into nothingness. The proverb quoted in v. 22 indicates that these men had never been changed. They had genuinely been drawn to Christ and had found much in the teaching of His messengers that fascinated them. But instead of submitting themselves to Him as Lord they tried to force Him into their systems and philosophies.

This description will be of value to us only as we first look to see how far we are tainted with the danger. It is so easy to demand that Christ conform to our emotional experiences—and others' also—or to our preconceived ideas of what they should be. If we are truly regenerated persons, this will lead merely to our making true Christianity revolve around an experience instead of Christ. All those who come to us with infallible recipes for blessing or signs of spirituality fall into this category. Alternately, we shall so stress one aspect of truth that the whole picture of Christ becomes distorted, or much truth is excluded from the framework we have so strictly drawn. Most of our sects and divisions are due to this. The great danger is that if we persist in this course, we shall find our sense of our importance so growing that the Person of Christ grows dimmer and marginal. Finally, we worship not Him but our idea of Him. Once that has happened only the grace of God can set limits to the evil into which we may fall.

When we have judged ourselves, we shall be better fitted to estimate Christian teachers around us. Beware of the man who makes himself the measuring-rod of truth and condemns all who do not conform. Beware of the man who exalts his experience above the Scriptures and who lets the moral law of God sit lightly on him. Beware of the man who seems to have one eye on his hearers' purses. Such men may be all right, but they stand in slippery places.

2 Peter 3.1-7   Scoffers

Peter now returns to the subject of the Second Coming. The very formality of v. 1 shows that ch. 2 was a digression, caused probably by his recent reading of *Jude*. Far more important than false teachers is our attitude to the Return. After all, if our attention is fixed on Christ and His Coming, we are not likely to be led astray by the false prophets and teachers. 'The commandment of the Lord' (2) refers to His statements in passages like Matt. **24,25**; Mark **13**; Luke **12**.32–48; **17**.22–37; **21**.5–36, with their repetition of the command to watch. 'Through your apostles': the epistles are full of admonitions reinforcing Christ's command. *1 and 2 Thessalonians* make it clear that the Second Advent must have played a large part in Paul's preaching and teaching in Thessalonica, cf. especially 1 Thess. **5**.1,2; 2 Thess. **2**.5.

There is no reason for identifying the 'scoffers' (3) with the false teachers of ch. **2**, though from the nature of their doctrines the Second Advent will have played little or no part in their thinking. 'Following their own passions' (3): cf. NEB 'and live self-indulgent lives'. The future implies that the scoffers are there and will continue, for, in company with the other apostles, Peter regarded the period of the Church as 'the last days', cf. 1 John **2**.18; Rom. **13**.12. These scoffers were men who wanted to live 'natural' lives bounded by the here and now. The concept of a God who can break into history and transform it is abhorrent to them. They may appeal to science as a justification but their god is man-made security.

21

Peter reminds them that in the Flood there was already a drastic recreating of the earth. His words are a warning against a minimizing of the Flood, but equally to read into them a meaning in conflict with all the evidence of science is foolish. Peter is not giving a new revelation of how *Genesis* is to be understood. Since the Flood, though a destruction, was a recreating, so the fire (7) will be a recreating, cf. Rev. **21.**1 (see notes).

Thought: If God broke into human history in Jesus, is there any reason why He should not do it again?

2 Peter 3.8-13   New Heavens and a New Earth

One of the oldest and most enduring delusions in the Church is the assumption that v. 8 gives us a yard-stick by which to measure God's time. Although archaeology has moved the indubitable evidence for the existence of *homo sapiens*, i.e. rational man as the Bible knows him, to before 8,000 B.C.—this is distinct from the claim that man-like creatures existed long before this—there are still many who are working on the basis of a Divine week, the last day of which is the Millennium (Rev. **20.**6). Had Peter meant anything like this he would have told his readers to stop thinking about the Second Coming. He means that since God's thoughts are not ours, we cannot interpret the 'soon' and 'quickly' of the Advent (see notes on Rev. **22.**6-12). If we grow tired waiting, let us remember that it is for the good of others.

We shall always be plagued by those who insist on finding in Scripture what is not there; it appeals to their vanity. So we are told that v. 10 together with vs. 7,12 refer to the blowing up of the earth by a nuclear explosion. Such an idea has its place in science fiction but not in sober Biblical exposition. The earth is God's, and neither Satan nor men can destroy it. What man's puny A and H bombs have shown is that God can burn up the world by using natural law as easily as He destroyed life on it by water.

The rendering 'hastening' (12) is linguistically possible but theologically an abomination! It is made quite clear in Scripture, cf. Mark **13.**32, that the day of the Coming lies in God's sovereignty, as is indeed implied by vs. 8 f. We must therefore follow the margin and NEB in rendering 'earnestly desiring' or 'look eagerly'.

Peter held the universal N.T. hope that this earth had its future in God's plans (13). The 'new heavens' are our atmosphere, not the

22

home of God, see note on Rev. **21.1**. 'Righteousness' is conformity
to God's will and standards.

*Thought: Time is part of man's nature, not God's. We must learn
to live in the present of God's activity.*

2 Peter 3.14-18   Life in the Light of the Coming

Peter sets two ideals before his readers. When Christ comes they
should be 'without spot or blemish' (14), cf. Eph. **5.27**. We are not
called to approximate to some abstract ideal. We are to let the Holy
Spirit work out the perfection of what we are. God made us all
different, and those differences are preserved in time and doubtless
in eternity. It is the flaws and stains for which God is not answer-
able that are to vanish. Then we are to be 'at peace' (14). Does the
thought of His Coming stir any fears in us? If so we are not at peace
with Him. Do our circumstances create anxiety in us? Then we do
not enjoy His peace, i.e. God's riches in Christ Jesus.

We sometimes complain that there are things hard to understand
in the Bible, as though God were small enough to be comprehended
by our formulas. Even Peter, the fisherman, found Paul, the scholar,
hard to understand at times (16). Where we find such difficulties
we should humbly tell God and our fellow men that we do not understand. Not so the proud man. He must find a meaning, even if he
twists the Scriptures and deduces doctrines dishonouring to God
and harmful to man (16 f.).

Peter's last word is 'grow' (18). That is one of the wonders of
being a Christian. We have all eternity to grow in, and eternity will
be insufficient to exhaust the wonders of God.

*Thought: Beware of controversy, for in controversy we are most
likely to twist Scripture to suit our views.*

Questions for further study and discussion on 2 Peter

1. What does 'faith' mean to Peter (**1.1,5**)? Compare his treatment
   with that of Paul and James.
2. What positive lessons concerning the understanding of the Bible
   can be gained from **1.20** f.? What other Scriptures are relevant
   to this subject?
3. Remembering the abundance of Christian cults, whose members
   visit from door to door, what should be (*a*) our attitude towards,
   and (*b*) method of dealing with, such false teachers?
4. In the light of ch. **3**, how should the doctrine of the Second
   Coming affect our living?

There is such a striking similarity between the introduction to this letter and the introduction to the Fourth Gospel (John 1.1–18) that it seems fairly certain that the letter was a covering document for the Gospel or that it was written shortly afterwards to develop certain concepts in it. The Gospel was written 'that you may believe . . . and that believing you may have life' (John 20.31), and this letter 'that you may know you have eternal life' (5.13). So the Gospel begins with the Word (John 1.1), and this letter with the Word of life (1), because by experiencing Him, Christians have come to know the One who has brought life (John 1.4).

Verse 1 amalgamates John 1.1 and 14. The one controversy in the fourth and fifth centuries that never received a satisfying answer was how God could become man; there should never have been controversy, because Matt. 11.27 gave due warning that an answer would not be found. No one stresses the deity of Christ more clearly than John, but equally His manhood is as clearly demonstrated. We have to lean back and try to let the wonder penetrate us. On the one hand He was 'the Word of life which was from the beginning' and on the other He was 'looked upon' and 'touched' (1).

When we think of 'eternal', or everlasting, 'life' (2) our tendency is to stress its endlessness, but for John it is, above all, that which was 'with the Father.' The presence of the tree of life in Eden, cf. Rev. 22.2, reminds us that man was not created immortal, but capable of not dying. Immortality belongs only to God (1 Tim. 6.16), and by giving Himself to us in Jesus Christ, He gives also immortality.

'Fellowship' (3) means having something in common. Christian fellowship is not based on common doctrine—that is the weakness of the denomination based on a detailed doctrinal basis, though this may be justified in a society which has been formed for a special purpose—but on sharing a common God and Saviour (3). 'We are writing' (4): the 'we' is emphatic. It is a letter from one who has had contact with the Incarnate Word during the days of His flesh ('we' is merely the normal style for letters, now mainly reserved for newspaper editors, though it is the more appropriate here, for John knew that all of his aposotolic brothers would have agreed with him). True unity in Christ produces true joy (4).

Question: How far do we know true fellowship with our fellow Christians?

We saw that fellowship with our fellow Christians depended on our fellowship with God. If there is that in us which God cannot share, there can be no true fellowship with Him. For the antithesis between light and darkness, see notes on Rev. **21.25**; **22.5**. To understand v. 5 we should think of the effects of a car's headlights, or even more, of a searchlight beam; with them we have either light or darkness; there is no intermediate zone. Man may hesitate to judge another, but for God the issue is clear-cut; a man is either in the dark or in the light. Because God is light, we can know Him and His will, but it involves our laying ourselves bare to the revealing light as well.

We have here a darkness-light parallelism, each on an ascending scale; on the dark side are vs. 6, 8, 10, on the light side vs. 7,9; **2.1**. First, we have the man who does not recognize the darkness, i.e. the lack of fellowship with God in which he lives (6). This is followed by the person claiming perfection at any given moment (8), and finally, in v. 10 there is the one who denies that he has ever sinned or shows any of its imperfections (the perfect tense in Greek). It is probable, however, that John is not thinking merely of the man who has persuaded himself that darkness is light and that he is mysteriously right and all others wrong, but also, of the man who in any given position claims complete rightness. With the ascending darkness of sin there is also the increasing power of Christ. In v. 7 we have the need of definite confession of the sin. Finally, in **2.1** we have the awakened sinner calling on Christ to deal with the serious situation in which he finds himself.

The way to fellowship with our brothers is through fellowship with God, but lack of fellowship with our brothers will reveal that we are out of fellowship with God (8). This verse also encourages us to avoid an undue preoccupation with our sins. Unless it is something serious we have persisted in, it is sufficient to walk in the light.

Thought: Concentrate on Christ, not on yourself.

1 John 2.1-6   Jesus Christ Our Advocate

John was an old man when he wrote his letter, so 'My little children' (1) comes appropriately from him. We shall see what he means by 'that you may not sin' when we deal with **3.9**; here we content ourselves with the remedy for sin. 'Advocate' is a linguistically accurate rendering of 'Paraclete', a term used in some of our hymns for the Holy Spirit. It is used of the Holy Spirit in John **14.**16,26; **15.**26;

16.7, and of the Lord Himself here. Obviously the same rendering should be used throughout if possible, for the Holy Spirit is 'another' Paraclete. The NEB does this with Advocate, although here it is placed in the margin. The Paraclete is the One whom one calls to one's side—Latin, *ad-vocatus*. This may be for help, for advice, for comfort, for representation. Behind all these lies the assumption that one hands over one's affairs completely to one's Advocate. He cannot act adequately unless one does. 'Jesus Christ the righteous': the implication of 'righteous' is that He completely meets the Father's standards.

'Expiation' (2): AV(KJV) 'propitiation'. The latter means to appease (God's) anger, the former to make good harm done. Neither is really an ideal translation, for in the N.T. the word and its cognates are used to express the Hebrew word *kipper* and its related forms in the O.T. This, translated atone, atonement, mercy-seat, has fundamentally the idea of covering (of sin). Hence the NEB rendering 'He is Himself the remedy for the defilement of our sins', and Phillips 'the One who made personal atonement for our sins', though not ideal, bring out the inner meaning.

Knowing Him (3,4), cf. John **17**.3, is virtually equivalent to walking in the light. Fellowship with God implies keeping His commandments. In addition, if we do hand our affairs over to Christ, it implies that we shall not be concerned with this or that commandment, but that His Word becomes an indwelling power (5). Then John passes over to a more personal expression. Walking in the light can be taken impersonally, but abiding in Him (6), cf. John **15**.4–10, indicates the believer's personal link with his Saviour. It is possible to stress Jesus as the pattern for our lives in a way that overshadows His atoning work, but for all that it is an essential part of the gospel.

Thought: There is nothing to fear, if we have handed everything over to Christ.

1 John 2.7-17   The Commandment of Love

Words divorced from events can be very empty things. So it is with our Lord's 'new commandment' (John **13**.34; **15**.12,17)—the fact that John does not specify it explicitly till **3**.11,23, shows the close link of *1 John* with the Gospel. It is not a new commandment, because we find it already in Lev. **19**.18. The very question in Luke **10**.29 shows how relatively shallow was the way in which it was understood. The moment Jesus linked it with Himself He transformed it, so that it became a new commandment. As the implications of

Christ's work became ever clearer in the Church (8), the darkness which hid the implications of Lev. **19**.18 was vanishing. 'He who . . . hates his brother' (9): the linguistic use of the O.T., e.g. Mal. **1**.2 f., and our Lord's teaching, e.g. Matt. **5**.43–48, make clear that no shadow-land is being left between love and hatred. Hatred is quite simply absence of love, and love must be understood in the light of Christ's life. Sin can be so evil, that it is sometimes very hard to hate the sin and love the sinner, especially when he loves his sin. So John makes his words turn on love to one's 'brother' (9–11) in faith.

John then gives what should be the characteristics of the developing Christian. To begin with there must be the knowledge of forgiveness (12) and of God's desire that men should be saved (13). The strength and courage of the Christian who has grown to man's stature are seen in his victory over the 'evil one' (13 f.) and his knowledge of God's will. Full maturity is shown by a true understanding of 'Him who is from the beginning' (13 f.), i.e. Jesus Christ. It would be well to compare these standards with much that is stressed today.

Wherever man is organized for business or pleasure without thought of God there we have the world (15). 'The things in the world' are man's works for his glory and pride, and not God's creation. No thing is in itself worldly; it is man's attitude, 'the lust of the flesh and the lust of the eyes and the pride of life', that makes it so. So while experience may show that certain things are dangerous or disadvantageous to the Christian, the vital question to ask is why he wants something, or why he wishes to do it. For Christ's teaching on the subject, see Matt. **6**.19–21, 24–34; Luke **16**.9–13.

Thought: Seek the things that are above, where Christ is.

1 John 2.18-27   The Anointing of the Holy Spirit

The Christian who has learnt how to look on society with the eyes of God is not likely to be misled by those false teachers whom John calls 'antichrists' (18). 'Anti' means 'in place of'; hence, antichrist may mean one who displaces Christ by claiming to be more important, or one who is the outspoken enemy of Christ. The latter is the sense in which we generally use the term and make it equivalent to 'the man of lawlessness' (2 Thess. **2**.3) or the 'beast' (Rev. **13**.1). Here John uses it for teachers who claimed to be Christians (19) but denied that Jesus was God's King (the Christ, 22). Since God is the Father primarily in virtue of Jesus Christ as His Son, and not in virtue of His creation of man, to deny the sonship of Jesus is to deny the fatherhood of God (22).

Scripture must be interpreted in its context. The AV(KJV) 'ye know all things' (20) is based on inferior manuscripts. To every true Christian the Holy Spirit gives an anointing and so he has an intuitive, inner knowledge of certain basic facts—'you all know'. This knowledge is not something that makes teaching and the study of the Scriptures unnecessary, nor does it introduce us to secrets of which the Bible says nothing. It is rather an intuitive knowledge that certain teaching is false (27), cf. John 10.5,27. One of the greatest difficulties for young Christians is when they find this inner light decried and they are virtually forced to assent to propositions which they know to be false. This inner light can easily be distinguished from the intellectualism that challenges established Christian doctrine. It will never deny the Scriptures; if it does, it is not of God.

It should be specially noted that John shows no distress at the fact that these antichrists were once church members (19). He was evidently confident that in the local church where Christ was Lord the false teacher would soon be too uncomfortable to stay for long. The mention of 'the last hour' (18, cf. notes on 1 Pet. 4.7) is intended to bring out that just as Jesus Christ brought the revelation of God to its earthly climax, so also it brings out the revelation of the climax of sin's rebellion.

Thought: Do not be afraid of being led by the Holy Spirit.

1 John 2.28—3.3   Our Hope

It is of little importance whether a man has much or little knowledge of Christ, whether his spiritual growth has been fast or slow. If he is abiding in Christ, the Spirit of Christ (cf. 1 Pet 1.11) is doing His transforming work in him, and he will welcome the returning Christ with all the simplicity of the child. It is the Christian who has chosen his own way that will 'shrink from Him in shame' (28), for the emptiness of his character will at once have become apparent. In v. 29; 3.7, we have one of the most important principles of the Christian life. We can teach correct doctrine to a parrot, but correct life comes only from the Holy Spirit.

Through our misunderstanding of the use of Father for God— see note on 2.22—we have largely lost the thrill of being able to say 'Father' to God, as indeed is revealed by so many of our public prayers. 'Children of God' (1) reflects Hebraic thought and implies that we reveal His character. We have become so hypnotized by correctness of doctrine that we fail to remember that it is correctness of life that matters. Since the world did not understand the Son of God, we cannot expect it to understand His sons and daughters, cf. John **15**.18 f.; Matt. **10**.24 f. There are very few who can predict the development of the child by looking at him; so it is with the Christian. There is little point in speculating about the transformed resurrection body; what is important is that we shall be like Him, 'like God in Christ' (Westcott), of the same nature. No wonder the one who has not allowed the Holy Spirit to do His work 'will shrink from Him in shame'.

No one can purify himself in the first place. That must be done by Christ as we trust in Him. But once we have been purified we can keep away from that which we know will defile us. The little child hauled out of the coal bunker cannot clean itself up, but it can keep away from the coal in future. No wonder John can extol the love of the Father. He who has really been gripped by this hope is not likely to be worried by worldliness. The glory of Christ causes the best of man's dreams to grow pale.

Thought: If you do not want to be like Christ, be assured that His likeness will never be forced on you.

Questions for further study and discussion on 1 John 1.1–3.3

1. What is the real basis of Christian fellowship? See **1**.7; 1 Cor. **1**.9; Phil. **1**.7; **2**.1; Tit. **1**.4.
2. Consider the place given to keeping commandments in the Christian life.
3. With the help of a concordance study the occurrence of the word 'world' in the N.T., and determine its various usages. How will our understanding of this word affect our daily living?
4. What is the relationship between the abiding of God's Word in us and our abiding in Him (ch.**2**)? Does the former make the latter automatic?
5. In view of **3**.2 f. what place should the Second Coming have in Christian proclamation?

1 John 3.4-10   The Reborn Man Cannot Sin

'Sin is lawlessness' (4): this does not mean that it is a breach of the law of Moses or of any specific command, cf. Rom. **5**.13 f. Sin is the setting up of oneself as one's own law and authority. 'It is the assertion of the selfish will against a paramount authority.'

The distinction between 'sins' and 'sin' (5) is vital to our understanding of the passage. Sins are the result of an inner principle of sin. The knowledge that Christ has borne our sins reconciles us to God, but our coming to Him and being reborn implies a treatment of the root rebellion of sin. One cannot abide in Him, or even know or see Him and remain rebellious against the law of God (6). The one 'born of God' (9)—the verb is perfect, i.e. the life continues and develops—will not continue in rebellion against God. Furthermore this birth means that something of 'God's nature' has been implanted in a person, so it is impossible that he should be in rebellion. But John fully shares Paul's attitude expressed in Rom. 7.7–25. The vanishing of the old nature awaits Christ's coming (3.2), and so falling short is bound to continue (1.8). See also 5.14–18. That this is the correct interpretation is seen by the fact that John sees sin particularly in two things: the consistent failure to try to achieve God's standards ('whoever does not do right'), and to 'love his brother' (10), in other words, it is a question of attitude rather than acts.

Human thought naturally expresses itself in alternatives, in either . . . or. Either a man is a sinner or sinless. Divine truths normally express themselves in both . . . and, or neither . . . nor. It is the latter we are dealing with here. Regenerate man is neither sinless nor a rebel against God. If a man is in rebellion against God, he should not expect his claim to be a Christian to be taken seriously. If we find him falling short of God's will, provided he does not deny the fact, it is rather a testimony to the greatness of God's miracle.

Thought: God transforms; He does not force His children into a mould.

1 John 3.11-24   Love in Action

While 'that we should love one another' (11) represents the goal of the message rather than its terms, we may well ask how far this could be affirmed of the normal presentation of the gospel today. Though none of those who reads this is likely ever to murder another, Christ has warned us that anger and insult rank along with it in God's sight (Matt. 5.22). So many of us criticize, impute motives, quietly stand in another's way because his life is an implicit criticism of ours, and his acts are more clearly blessed than ours (12). We should not wonder if the world hates us (13); indeed the wonder should be, if it does not. But what are we to say of the petty hatred and spite of our fellow Christians? We have to hold in spiritual balance the truths that hatred, i.e. lack of love, is murder (15), and that love is not a natural thing but the result of rebirth (14). The love John is writing about is Christ's love (16; 4.19). 'He laid down His life' (16): the translation is unsatisfactory. He gave up His self and this culminated in death (Phil. 2.5–8). Similarly, we have to give up our selves; whether this ends in premature death—unlike Jesus we have to die!—or not depends entirely on God's will. 'The world's goods' (17): the NEB is more likely to be correct with 'enough to live on' than Phillips with 'the well-to-do man'. The giving out of our superfluity is taken for granted; it is the lowering of our own standard of living that is being considered. Note, too, that John is not writing about turning away the beggar, but of responding to what our eyes have seen. Love sharpens vision.

The fruit of love is confidence (19; 4.18). The Greek of vs. 19,20 is far from easy. The sense seems to be that if our heart, i.e. our conscience, condemns us, (there is no suggestion that the condemnation is mistaken), then the knowledge that we love the brethren enables us confidently to trust in the grace of God, who has given us new life, for He is greater than any shortcoming of ours. On the other hand we do not have confidence for unfettered asking (22) until the voice of conscience is satisfied (21), for we could be asking amiss. The summary of the O.T. law (Mark 12.29–31) is here rephrased as trust in Jesus Christ ('believe in the name') and love of the brethren (23). There is a double abiding. Our abiding in Him depends on our doing His will. His abiding in us is by His Spirit (24).

Thought: Tragic is the plight of the man who resists the urge of the Spirit to unite him to Christ.

1 John 4.1-12   Love is Supreme

At the end of ch. 3 John mentioned the Holy Spirit for the first time, even though He may be implicit in a passage like 2.20. The reason immediately becomes obvious. Then as now there were those who preferred the 'gifts of the Spirit' to the more costly 'fruit of the Spirit'. They might not show much love, but they did display spiritual gifts, in this case prophetic (1). John did not deny the fact of spirit activity, for there are spirits other than the Holy Spirit (1). The acknowledgement of the Incarnation was a sure test (2), for apparently it had brought the spirits in a special way under the control of the name of Jesus Christ (Mark 16.17; Acts 19.13). 'The spirit of antichrist' (3): see note on 2.18. Stress on these phenomena, even if they are superficially harmless and orthodox, deflects attention from Christ. Their attractiveness is that 'they are of the world' (5), i.e. they appeal to the natural man. Ultimately, we may know the validity of a teacher's message by those whom he attracts (6).

John then dismisses these people by returning to the subject of love, the primacy of which remains absolute, cf. 1 Cor. **13**.1–3, and it is the one certain test of a man's standing before God. Snaith in writing of the love of God in the N.T. has called it election love, because it is always seen in action. So here, too, the love of God is characterized by God's sending (9), cf. John 3.16. God's love is always prior and basic (10). One of the basic stresses in *Hosea* lies just here. Since God had included all Israel in His covenant love, for one Israelite to wrong another was to deny the relation of covenant love that God had set up. 'Love me, love my dog' is a down-to-earth version of what is being stressed here.

It goes further. 'No man has ever seen God' (12): we know Him by what He has done for us, above all in Jesus Christ, in whom He became visible, and by what He has worked in our fellow men. So long as our love to God is a matter of feelings towards Him, or even expressed in the living of a moral life, it is a static love. Once it shows itself in action towards those whom God has loved, it 'is perfected in us'.

1 John 4.13-21   God is Love

At this point John pauses and picks up some of the strands of his message. Verse 13 looks back to 3.24; v. 14 to 1.2; 2.2; v. 15 to 3.23 f. The basis of everything is that the Father sent and the Son saved. We accept this in our confession of Jesus as the Son of God, and to us the proof of this is the possession of the Holy Spirit.

'Thus we have come to know and believe the love which God has for us' (16a, NEB): the climax of our union with God is a fusion of experience and faith, not concerned with abstract theology but with the expression of God's love, not merely to me, but also to others.

A new section begins with 'God is love', cf. NEB. We may not qualify this in any way, but equally we may not preach it to those who have not experienced it. Since it is an abstract statement, we must make it concrete in Christ and in our own lives, otherwise men will interpret it by their own concepts of love. Where man and God are linked in love, the love of God flows to man, and through him out to his fellow man and back to God, thus causing 'the day of judgement' (17) to take on another aspect. Even in this world we show by our love that we are like Him. To those who are strangers to God, or who have just come into living contact with Him, we have to bring 'theologies of the atonement' to demonstrate that Christ's death was more than just the tragic death of a very good and noble man. Caught up in the sphere of love both doubts and fears vanish.

'There is no fear in love' (18) does not exclude the possibility of God's discipline or even of the tendency of the old nature to shrink back. 'Punishment' here is almost fear of the consequences, for it is retributory punishment and not discipline, cf. Heb. 12.5–11, that is being considered. In God's love this is excluded for those who are linked to Him by the bonds of love. There is not even the fear of our love breaking down, for it is His love (19). Man's love can discriminate, God's does not, so to hate my brother is to make a mockery of the love to God I claim (20). In any case my attitude towards the one I see daily is a sure token of my attitude towards the One I have never seen.

1 John 5.1-12 The Three Witnesses

'Christ' in Greek is not a proper name but a title, and a most unusual one for John's contemporaries. The challenge is to believe that Jesus is God's Messiah, i.e. His King and Representative. Once again we have the stress that love is a relationship within the family (1). As such it is not primarily emotional but derives its nature from God. If we have the right relation to God and 'obey His commandments' (2), our love to God's fellow children will look after itself, because obedience is a sign of our love to God. Obedience is 'not burdensome' (3), because we share a common character with God, cf. Matt. 11.30. Yet we may never think that the Christian life is something merely automatic. There is the continuous conflict with the world, which demands the continued use of 'our faith' (4), which must give Jesus His full position (5).

The verse numbering of RSV hides the fact that v. 7 of AV(KJV) has been omitted, certainly correctly. The statement about the three witnesses in heaven is found in Latin sources in the 5th century, but no Greek manuscript before the 13th century contains it. With its omission we find the justification for our confession of Jesus as the Son of God. John's thought is hard to follow in detail, and there is point in Law's view (*The Tests of Life*) that we have 'a summary . . . intended to recall fuller oral exposition'.

While 'water and blood' (6) have some relation to John 19.34, the different order shows that primarily it refers to His baptism and death. In contrast, the reference to the Spirit is in the present and must refer to His witness in the Church. So the 'three witnesses' (8) are the Spirit (mentioned first!), Baptism and the Lord's Supper. The blessing on the sacraments, when rightly used, from generation to generation, shows that God has approved of them, and so the three are God's testimony (9). Where men accept God's objective testimony, they receive a subjective inner testimony as well. Men may disbelieve us with impunity, but to disbelieve God is to charge Him with being a liar. To believe is life, to disbelieve is death (12).

Thought: In your witness do not place yourself between God and man.

1 John 5.13-21 Sin unto Death

In the concluding section of the letter, John brings together a number of his main points. Certainty of salvation ('eternal life') is not a necessity, but it certainly makes the Christian walk easier and more triumphant (13). When we love (3.21–23) we shall know the will of the Beloved, and so we shall ask according to His will and obtain it (14). Neither need we wait for the visible answer (15).

It is a pity that the RSV and NEB do not keep 'a sin unto death' (16 f.), for as Westcott points out, the Greek means 'tending to death' —only God can ultimately classify sin. John is writing about believers (16), and the Roman Catholic concept of mortal sin, i.e. one that will bring a man to hell, if not repented of, has no Scriptural justification. Especially in the light of 1 Cor. **11**.30 there is no reason why we should not take death and life literally. All sin within the Church is unspeakably serious for it mars the witness of the body of Christ. In the story of Ananias and Sapphira we have God visiting such persons with death (Acts **5**.1–11). Paul envisages the notorious sinner as handed over to Satan for the destruction of the flesh (1 Cor. **5**.5). Because of the serious lack of discipline in the Church, we seldom see John's teaching being applied, but this does not alter God's attitude towards the sin of Christians.

The mention of this possibility of sin causes John to stress once again that it is really a contradiction in terms (18). The combination, however, makes clear that we must regard the state of not sinning as the normal, not as the impossible. The child can deny his parentage, but cannot undo it.

Because there was a time when it appeared that the Church had Christianized Europe and many of its colonies, the distinction between the true Church and the world became blurred. It remains

34

true, however, that the world (see note on 2.15) is always in opposition to God, and whether it knows it or not, under the control of Satan.

'To know Him who is true' (20): cf. Rev. **19.11**. There 'reliable' is the better rendering, but here 'real' (NEB) is perhaps best, for it is contrasted with 'idols' (21). The Greek word implies an image without inner reality, or a shadow. God is real; man's desires are vain shadows.

Thought: 'On Christ, the solid Rock, I stand.'

Questions for further study and discussion on 1 John 3.4–5.21

1. Starting from 3.4 collect and analyse the Biblical descriptions of sin. What do these teach us about man?
2. In the light of **3.**16b (cf. Acts **20.**24; Phil. **2.**30; Rev. **12.**11) how can we express the radical character of Christian love in our present environment?
3. In 4.2 John goes beyond the simple test of 1 Cor. **12.**3; do we need a more elaborate test than John's in the present-day Church?
4. What does it mean to have victory over the world (5.4)? Look up 'overcome' in a concordance.
5. Does the Bible make any excuses for unbelief? How should our answer to this affect our evangelism?

2 John 1-6 The Primacy of Love

Neither contents nor tradition give any idea of the date of this short letter, or of its recipient. The style suggests a date near that of *1 John*. If that is so, the worsening position of the Church in the Roman empire would explain its essential anonymity.

'The elder' (1): cf. 1 Pet. **5.**1. John is not claiming apostolic authority. 'The elect lady': the position might explain the omission of the name, but contrast 3 John 1. The use of the same term in v. 13, however, suggests strongly that a personified local church is intended. This is strengthened by his statement that all who know the truth share his outlook. 'The truth' (2) is, of course, Christ, cf. John 14.6. 'Grace' (3) is God's free covenant love; 'mercy', or better, 'compassion', is His understanding of the Church's position and weakness as it faces the increasing hostility of the Roman power; 'peace' is the inner quiet from having all the resources of God at one's disposal.

'Some of your children' (4): this otherwise strange remark becomes clear, if we understand it to mean that John had met some of the recipient church's members when they were on their travels. In this case it does not imply that the others had lapsed. John was living at a time when false teachers were rife, and so the churches were making their first steps towards tighter organization and formulation of doctrine, to exclude them. John approves, but he sees the danger. So he urges that first things be placed first, i.e. love. Where there is true love the false teacher will find himself ignored. 'That you follow love' (6): if this were the correct translation it would mean seeing Jesus as the personification of love. The AV(KJV) 'that ye should walk in it', is, however, correct, or as expressed by the NEB 'to be your rule of life'. Since it is Divine love John is writing about, it is neither weak nor sentimental. It will not compromise nor call evil good, nor false true.

Thought: Love is a soil in which falsehood cannot grow.

2 John 7-13 Plague Carriers

For v. 7, cf. notes on 1 John 2.18; 4.3. In one way or another the false teacher tries to diminish the importance of Christ in order to stress his doctrine. Whenever anyone suggests that his views should take priority in a Christian's life and thinking, he has become an antichrist. Unbalanced doctrine, even if not positively false, leads to unbalanced thought and action, and this will lead to an unbalanced reward, i.e. something will be missing (8). 'Anyone who goes ahead' (9): Phillips gets the meaning excellently with, 'The man who is so "advanced" that he is not content with what Christ taught.' Where true love exists, there will be the willingness to believe that God's love has revealed all that is necessary, and that, in any case, ideas that only puzzle my fellow Christians have no real place in Christian teaching. We generally assume they are too uneducated, too conservative, too unintelligent (how loving!) to understand; love would suggest that it is their spirituality that makes them turn from my ideas. The refusal of greeting (10) shows that John is not writing about the casual stranger, whose views would be unknown, but about the known teacher claiming the right to propagate his views. To receive him would be as senseless as welcoming the carrier of plague or other major infectious disease. Probably John was thinking of certain teachers going round the area, but he did not wish to put too much on paper, lest the letter fall into the hands of the authorities. The man who has given himself to the perversion of truth will also twist the fact that I have given him hospitality, and will claim that my action has given him a testimonial of respectability.

It is not always wise to write too much. Very much harm has been done to Christian work in the mission field and in lands hostile to Christianity by enthusiastic reports that have fallen into the wrong hands. So John was prepared to leave what else was to be said until he could visit the church to which he had sent his warning.

Question: Do my pet views enhance the glory of Christ?

3 John 1–8   A Hospitable Home

There are no grounds for separating this short letter widely in time from *1* and *2 John*. In other words it was probably written towards the end of the first century. 'Elder' (1): see notes on 2 John 1; 1 Pet. **5**.1. The apostles were authorities on doctrine, but they could not impose their will on an already established church. John writes with the authority due to the senior elder of the church in Ephesus— at least so tradition says—but that does not give him power over another church. 'Gaius' was a common name at the time. Three or possibly four other men of that name are mentioned in the N.T., and we can hardly identify him with any of them. The salutation suggests that he may have been ill, and even that he may have been involved in some difficulties. John had no doubt of his spiritual state. Gaius may well have been a convert of John's (4). 'The truth of your life' (3) does not refer to doctrinal purity, but to a harmony between words, actions and character.

Here we have the opposite of 2 John 10 f. For reasons connected with Diotrephes (9) the church in which Gaius was a member had not welcomed wandering preachers as they should. Gaius had evidently taken them in and been taken to task by the church for so doing. John expresses the hope that he will so do again (6), for they refused to accept any form of payment from the 'heathen' to whom they had preached. The obvious distinction between them and the false teachers was that they were not seeking to influence the church at all; they were missionaries to the heathen around. The regulations of Matt. **10**.5–13 could apply only partially because they were preaching, not to God-fearing Jews, but to idolatrous pagans. If it is asked why the church that sent them out did not provide for their needs, it may be suggested that it was often inadvisable for such travellers to carry much money. Until the local synagogue rejected Paul's teaching, he could rely on Jewish hospitality, but those days were long past.

Thought: We do not have to preach to share the preacher's work.

3 John 9-15 The Church Dictator

The trouble in the church was due to Diotrephes (9), 'who wants to be head of everything' (Phillips). No false doctrine is attributed to him; it was simply that he felt he had to have a finger in every pie. It is not clear whether the 'something' John had written to the church was a protest to the church for the way it had behaved or a few lines commending the travelling preachers. Since he is not likely to have written so lightly about a formal protest, it was probably the latter. Diotrephes probably objected to the fact that the letter had not been addressed to him personally and that he had not been consulted in advance. He will have had no objection to the preachers as such.

Diotrephes was not yet a bishop; they developed later. His authority was limited, and the only way he could counteract John's lines of commendation was to slander him. This has remained to this day one of the most effective ways of undermining true spiritual authority. There can be little doubt that the NEB is correct in v. 10 with 'and tries to expel them from the congregation'. There is no evidence that Gaius had been excommunicated, though Diotrephes would doubtless have been pleased to get rid of him. While John could not order the church about, he had the right to expose what had happened, when he visited the church. The 'authority' (9) which Diotrephes had not recognized, was to commission the preachers. 'Demetrius' (12) had probably resisted him and been bitterly attacked.

Diotrephes has always been in the church, and has probably done more harm than false teachers. There is always the willingness to let the 'willing horse' carry more than his share of the church burdens. This, of course, robs the less gifted of their opportunities of service. Sometimes the 'willing horse' is motivated purely by the spirit of service; then he normally has a break-down. Sometimes it is the drive to get his nose in everywhere. If this is allowed, the day comes when he is felt to be indispensable and he becomes a dictator. Then he grumbles because no one seems willing to pull his weight!

Thought: 'Through love be servants of one another' (Gal. **5**.13).

Jude 1-7 There is Judgement on Godlessness

The bulk of this short letter is reproduced in 2 Pet. **2**, and the notes on that chapter should be referred to. In our study of it we must remember that we are dealing with two phenomena which need not be linked. It is a pungent attack on men who, while genuinely attracted to certain features of Christianity, had no real claim to the name. Today they are represented by some of the modern cults and certain theosophical groups. Then they represented a widespread antinomian, anti-moral movement, which was not confined to Christian circles, though they found the rapidly growing, enthusiastic groups a useful base. Such an outlook is sweeping over us again today, but for the most part it has no interest in Christianity, or the churches.

Jude, cf. Mark **6**.3, is Judas or Judah, the third of Jesus' brothers; apart from this letter nothing is known of him. Hegesippus tells us that his grandsons were brought before the Emperor Domitian (A.D. 81–98) as members of the House of David, and hence possible rallying points for Jewish disaffection. When he found they were mere peasants, he sent them home. The NEB gives the sense better in v. 1, 'to those whom God has called, who live in the love of God the Father and in the safe keeping of Jesus Christ.'

Jude had been wanting to write to his unnamed readers when a sudden danger made it necessary (3). 'To contend': there is no necessary connection with physical fighting in the word. 'Once for all': hence new ideas and revelations just cannot be true. These men (4) found acceptance in Christian circles by hiding their views at first. The foretelling of their coming is found in passages like Matt. **24**.5,24. 'Our only Master and Lord': Master is a strong word, used in 1 Pet. **2**.18 for a slave-owner. Only here and in 2 Pet. **2**.1 is it applied to Jesus Christ, to show how wicked their action was. Their denial was by a life and teaching completely contrary to His.

He said their doom had been foretold (4), and this he demonstrates by listing some of the judgements on similar men in the past. As Paul makes clear in 1 Cor. **10**.6–8, one of the chief sins of the Israelites in the wilderness was immorality. We know from Jewish writings that 'the angels' (6) were above all those mentioned in Gen. **6.2,4,** cf. note on 1 Pet. **3.**19 f. On the basis of Gen. **19.**4–11, it is assumed in Jewish tradition that the sin of Sodom and Gomorrah was above all unnatural vice, though this is hardly borne out by Ezek. **16.**49 f. 'Eternal fire' means fire that blotted out the cities for ever.

Thought: The best way of contending for the truth is living it.

Jude 8-16   The Ungodliness of the Ungodly

Jude calls the doctrines of these teachers dreams (8); they had no solid basis. They degraded the human body, ignored authority ordained by God and insulted those to whom God had given glory by the position He had granted them. One feature of Jude is his familiarity with Jewish apocalyptic and pseudepigraphic writings. In v. 9 he quotes from *The Assumption of Moses.* It is immaterial whether it is factual; this is how one should behave in the presence of God's great officials. Satan acted as a sort of public prosecutor, cf. Job **1.**6–12; **2.**1–6; Zech. **3.**1–5; Luke **22.**31. These men had destroyed their higher nature by their dreams, and so they had become like animals to be destroyed by their passions. Cain committed murder because his brother's life rebuked his (see note on 1 John **3.**12). For Balaam, see note on 2 Pet. **2.**15; he was willing to flout God's will for money. Korah rebelled against God-given authority (Num. **16.**1–35).

'These are blemishes on your love feasts' (12): this is the way it is taken in 2 Pet. **2.**13, where an almost identical Greek word is used. There is, however, much to be said for taking the word here as meaning 'hidden reefs', hence Phillips 'these men are a menace'. The picture is of them sitting in the love feasts of the local church threatening the spiritual life of those around them by their conversation and selfish conduct. Like 'waterless clouds' they have a promise of good things but give nothing; 'fruitless trees in late autumn' will bear no fruit, cf. Mark **11.**12–14,20, and none in the future because they have no roots. The 'sea' (13) is the O.T. symbol for chaos and lawlessness, cf. Isa. **57.**20. The 'wandering stars' are probably comets.

In vs. 14,15 we have a quotation from *The Book of Enoch,* a Jewish pseudepigraph. There is no importance in the fact that this is an extra-canonical book, for Jude could have easily found similar statements in the canon. The tense is the prophetic perfect, i.e. that foretold is so certain, that it can be described as though it had already happened. It was the constant use of 'ungodly' that commended the passage to Jude. They were 'loud-mouthed boasters' with small people, but flatterers of the great.

Thought: Jesus Christ died for these people also.

Jude 17-25   Our Defence against the Godless

Such predictions had been given by the apostles—Jude does not claim the rank—quite frequently; this is the force of the tense in v. 18. Examples are Acts 20.29; 1 Tim. 4.1; 2 Tim. 3.1 f.; 4.3. We have the general sense of them in v. 18. One of the characteristics of such people is the divisions they cause (19). Since they care only for themselves, they care nothing for the unity of the Church. Though they are completely unspiritual, they claim to be spiritual teachers.

The defence against such teachers is fourfold. Our faith (20) is only the beginning. We have to build up a rounded Christian character on it. Then we must 'pray in the Holy Spirit', cf. Rom. 8.26 f. This means that we must allow God's Spirit to mould our thoughts, cf. 1 John 5.14 f. 'Keep yourselves in the love of God' (21): the love of God is always there, but we can cut ourselves from it by sin. A thin blind can shut out the sunlight. Above all, there is the waiting for the return of Christ. It has a strange power to bring matters into true perspective, and inspire us to try to save others.

The final doxology faces facts squarely. On the one hand is man in his imperfection, who can be helped up when he is in danger of falling, and kept unblemished though not perfect; on the other hand is God with all glory, majesty, dominion and authority. The two are linked by Jesus Christ, the God-man.

Prayer: Lord, teach us to see Thee in Thy greatness and man in his smallness.

Questions for further study and discussion on 2 and 3 John and Jude

1. At least one modern commentator has criticized the stern attitude of 2 John 9–11: do you think this attitude ought to be practised today? If so, how?
2. What was there about Gaius that especially called forth John's love for him (3 John 1)?

3. Study the N.T. teaching on Christian hospitality and support (3 John 5–8).
4. How should the local church deal with a modern Diotrephes? What does the N.T. teach on church discipline?
5. Note the strong denunciations of Jude: what is the right balance between denunciation of sinners and attempts to save them, and how do we preserve it?

Revelation

INTRODUCTION

When it is rightly understood, the *Revelation* is one of the most important books in the Bible. Though it was not the last to be written, it fittingly stands at the end of the N.T., for in many ways it picks up themes, which have their start in *Genesis*, and brings them and others to a focus.

There are three main recognized methods of interpreting the book, though each is capable of almost infinite subdivision. The Praeterist sees the whole book, except the final couple of chapters, as referring to and fulfilled in the time in which it was written. The Historicist sees the history of the Church depicted in broad outline from ch. 4 onwards. The Futurist considers chs. 2,3 to be an outline of Church history, while everything from ch. 4 onwards is still future. The first two are obviously inadequate, the third must wait for the future before it can be judged, but its treatment of chs. 2,3 does not give us much confidence in its attempts to peer into the future. Best is to accept the opening words as a guide and to look on it as 'a revelation of Jesus Christ'. These notes adopt this method, though the obviously future elements are treated as such. Only rarely are the three schools of interpretation mentioned.

The language of the book is very largely symbolic. This symbolism is sometimes taken from contemporary apocalyptic writings, more often from the O.T., especially *Ezekiel* and *Daniel*. Both the nature of symbolism and its use are made clear in the notes.

There are no real grounds for doubting that the John who

42

wrote the book was the apostle of the same name. It is more likely to have been written in the reign of the Emperor Domitian (A.D. 81–96) than in that of Nero (54–68).

Revelation 1.1-8   Greetings from the Triune God

Fundamentally 'the Preacher' was correct in maintaining that 'there is nothing new under the sun' (Eccles. 1.9), for neither the nature of God, of Satan, nor of man changes. Hence the same patterns keep on recurring, though doubtless they may reach a climax before the Second Advent. This justifies the stress on 'the time is near' (3). Jesus is the Coming One, and Christians are intended to be kept awake by seeing signs of that coming in the things that happen. Hence it would be unfair to say that the Praeterist or Historicist was spiritually wrong in his interpretation.

We may look on Jesus in two ways. He is the eternal Word of God (John 1.1–18), but He is also that Word once in time made flesh for us, keeping His humanity for ever. It is these two aspects that are united in this portion; in v. 2 'word' should probably have a capital letter. Before Greek philosophical skill led to our formulation of the doctrine of the Trinity, there was really no other way of expressing this mystery. God as the one 'who is to come' (8) is Jesus Christ (7). If God is the A and the Z, the modern English for 'Alpha and Omega' (8), Jesus calls Himself 'the first and the last' (17), cf. also 22.12 f. For 'the seven spirits' (4), cf. Isa. 11.2; the Holy Spirit is meant, but Hebrew thought allowed each of His attributes to be considered separately; seven is the number of perfection and completeness. There is nothing outside His power and influence.

The Greek of *Revelation* is most unusual and it is likely that we should take v. 6 as in Exod. 19.6, to which it obviously refers. We are not merely under God's sovereignty, the force of 'kingdom', cf. v. 9, but we have also the right of unhindered access to Him, the force of priests. Zech. 12.10 refers only to the Jew, but v. 7 extends the truth to all, for in the sight of God all are responsible for the crucifixion. For 'the clouds' (7); it means He comes from God as God's representative.

Thought: The main thoughts of Revelation are so understandable that there is a blessing on its public reading.

If, as seems almost certain, *Revelation* was written c. A.D. 90 during Domitian's persecution, John will have been getting on for eighty, when he was condemned to hard labour in the quarries of Patmos. This must have been physically crushing for a man of his age, but though he had no day off and little leisure, he could still be 'in the Spirit' (10). It is unlikely that the Lord's day means Sunday; it corresponds rather to the Day of the Lord in the O.T., meaning the period in which the judgements of God are abroad in the world as He sets up His universal rule. While the visions may perhaps span a long period in the history of the Church, they are looking to and preparing for the Second Coming. 'The seven churches' (11) are literal, and a Bible map will show that they come in the natural order for a messenger carrying the letters; seven, however, indicates that we may expect to find all forms of church experience paralleled here. The force of 'angels' (20) is not clear; it may mean their guardian angels, cf. Matt. **18.**10. Neither bishops nor the churches' messengers to John carries conviction.

The description of the glorified Christ is almost completely symbolic. 'One like a son of man' (13), cf. Dan. **7.**13—human, yet with heavenly glory. 'A long robe', cf. Isa. **6.**1; the length of His garment showed His dignity as king and priest. The 'girdle' by its material showed the wearer's rank; that it was 'round His breast' means that it was not holding up His robe, i.e. He was at rest, His work done. 'His hair' (14), cf. Dan. **7.**9; He is simultaneously one like a son of man and the Ancient of Days, depicted with white hair because He has existed from all eternity. The description of His eyes reflects Dan. **10.**6; for Him to see means purification or destruction. 'His feet' (15) showed that there had been no defilement from the paths of earth He had trodden. 'Like the sound of many waters' (15), cf. Ezek. 1:24; to stand by a rockbound coast in a storm or a mighty waterfall and let the noise possess you will give the sense. The 'two-edged sword' (16) reminds us of Heb. **4.**12 f. The 'right hand' (17) is a symbol of strength and protection, so it also imparts strength. 'I died' (18): better, 'I became dead' (RV), for it refers to a deliberate and voluntary action. 'Hades' (Heb. *Sheol*) is not hell, but where the souls of the dead await the resurrection and judgement.

Question: How great is Jesus to you?

The operative word in all the seven letters is 'I know'. Our knowledge of ourselves is at the best distorted by self-interest, ignorance and prejudice. We see in part and we know in part. Christ's knowledge is complete, objective and constructive. He rebukes so as to restore.

The church in Ephesus, founded by Paul, and later, John's home, had all the makings of an ideal church. It not only did what it should, but continued when the ground was stony and the going hard. It was not influenced by outward appearances, but tested the claims of those who claimed special gifts and position (2, 'apostles'). But though it had not grown weary in well doing (3), the original motives and driving force had gone (4). The rendering 'abandoned' (4) should make us sit up. The AV(KJV) 'lost' may make us think of a very human cooling of ardour, something that is inevitable when love is thought of as mainly or entirely a matter of feelings. But here was the deliberate adoption of a lower standard. The works had ceased to be the outpouring of love and had become essentially legalistic, for the demands of love were proving too costly. Where this happens in a church, it is near spiritual death.

The root of the matter was still there, however, as was seen in their treatment of the Nicolaitans (6), i.e. the followers of one Nicolaus, of whom absolutely nothing is known. Certain popular guesses are best disregarded. That love was there was shown by their hating, neither the heretics nor their teaching, but their works. A teaching, however plausible, which produces the wrong results, must be false; if the results are right, its errors must be marginal. Love will always detect the loveless life, even if it is bewildered by the loveless teaching.

'To him who conquers' (7): to be accounted righteous by faith is only the beginning of a life terminating with the victor's crown of righteousness (2 Tim. 4.8). Eternal life comes through the act of faith, but the rewards through a life of faith. The conqueror knows he will be a member of the Church glorified, the new Jerusalem, where the tree of life is (22.2).

Thought: What excuse will I give Christ for failure?

Smyrna was a much smaller town than Ephesus, and so the church there, even though it was probably much smaller, was much more obvious to its neighbours and correspondingly persecuted. As a result they were poor (9), probably in numbers, spiritual gift and possessions, things that so often go together. So Jesus reminded them of His victory (8), and that they were rich (9), for to the poor in spirit comes the guarantee of living under the kingly rule of God (Matt. 5.3).

Evidently their chief difficulties came from the local Jews. Satan is the accuser and slanderer—the meaning of *diabolos* (Devil). So apparently they had both accused the church and slandered it, cf. Acts 13.45,50; 14.2,19; 17.5-8,13; 18.12 f. For the denial that they were really Jews (9), cf. Rom. 2.28 f. This kind of attitude is far too common among Christians, when they speak of movements they dislike or reject. We picture them as we feel they should be, and we allow report to feature as fact.

Even though it is usual for Church histories to describe the nearly three hundred years of persecution by the Roman authorities under ten major heads, this does not justify us for equating the church in Smyrna with that of the period of persecution. Probably the significance of the 'ten days' (10) is that the Lord of the Church both gives it over to persecution and so controls the persecutors, that He can foretell the time of its ending before it begins.

Because Christ was raised from the dead, physical death should have no terrors for us, even if it can be very painful. The death to be feared is the second, spiritual death (11, cf. Matt. 10.28). There are Christians who, though they will not be burnt, will as it were be singed. Probably no one knows the full implication of being saved 'but only as through fire' (1 Cor. 3.15). Though there is no suggestion of purgatory in it, it certainly implies more than the loss of one's life-work.

Thought: The poor church enjoys the riches of no condemnation.

Revelation 2.12-17   Hard By Satan's Throne

Pergamum had once been the important capital of an independent little kingdom, but now its political importance was merely a memory and it had been outshone commercially by Ephesus. It remained famous for the temple of Zeus which topped its hill—'Satan's throne' (13). Life was dominated by it, and its priests had early claimed the life of Antipas, who is otherwise unknown. In such surroundings there had to be a clear-cut response to the official paganism of the city, which presented no difficulty to the true believer. More subtle by far was the suggestion that he should recognize the hidden truth in it, an attitude that is all too prevalent in theoretical missionary thinking today.

The mention of 'Balaam' (14, see Num. **25**.1–9,16–18; **31**.8,16) shows that the syncretism they were threatened by was a grosser form of Gnosticism, in which the initiates were encouraged to indulge in sins of the flesh to show that they had risen above the restraints of the Law. If you meet such a one, for they still exist, shun him; he is a carrier of spiritual plague. The mention in the same context of the 'Nicolaitans' (15, cf. v. 6) suggests that Nicolaus' teaching was also a Gnostic one, though probably not so gross. When a church permits such things, God's judgement on the sinner will affect it as well (16).

'The hidden manna' (17) in its literal meaning looks back to the jar of manna placed in the Ark (Exod. **16**.33; Heb. **9**.4), the contents of which were controlled solely by God. In the context we have true spiritual secrets, 'the name' and the nourishment, in contrast to the spurious wisdom and secrets of the Gnostics. For some there is always a very strong pull towards the idea that there are special teachings and meanings in the Bible which can be appreciated only by the *élite*. When such teaching is met, we should not stop to ask whether it is true—though it is well to remember that the unprovable has little to commend it—but whether it brings us to closer personal intimacy with God.

Thought: Beware of those who wish to reduce the Bible to a book of doctrine; it is the record of God's mighty acts explained by God's prophets.

Revelation 2.18-29 A Mixed Church

The church in Thyatira was a strange mixture. On the one hand it excelled that in Ephesus in its Christian life and labour (19, cf. vs. 2,3), because their mounting scale showed that their love had not grown cold (cf. v. 4). Had Lydia (Acts **16**.14) perhaps returned home? On the other hand it had gone further than any of the other churches in yielding to the immoral Gnostic teaching around (20).

'Jezebel' was evidently one of those women with pronounced

47

psychic powers who have a strange influence on otherwise level-headed Christians. The name given her—it is hardly likely to have been her real one—links her with Ahab's wife, a lady who showed sufficient respect for the God of Israel to let her children's names include His and who doubtless attended her husband's worship of Jehovah, but whose real religion was the gross nature worship of Tyre with its deification of sex. In Ephesus and Pergamum it is a syncretistic corruption of Christianity that is condemned, but here the adoption of another religion —'adultery' (22)—which would involve suffering and death for its propagators and followers.

It is impossible to be sure whether 'the deep things of Satan' (24) refers to 'Jezebel's' teaching or to some other form of Gnostic aberration. There are those who delight in penetrating beyond the veiled hints in the Bible about the powers of evil that surround us. At the best their teaching deflects our attention from Jesus Christ, at the worst it defiles heart and mind. There is normally spiritual pride behind it. Have you noticed that the O.T. never describes the heathen religions that surrounded and influenced Israel? Not evil but its remedy should be our interest.

He who conquers in the Thyatiran situation is the man whose heart and mind are satisfied and filled with his Lord. So his reward is that he lives in the hope of the coming dawn (cf. v. 28 with 22.16), and that he shares in his Lord's rule (26,27). This point will be of special importance in our study of ch. 12.

The picture of the rod of iron is taken from Psa. 2.9. We must choose whether we are to be shepherded and defended by the Lord's rod (Psa. 23.4) or broken in pieces by it.

Revelation 3.1-6 A Dead Church

Doctors are given to post-mortems to discover the cause of death, and they are doubtless very often justified. Though we very often indulge in them, post-mortems on spiritual deaths seldom serve a good purpose, and so we have none on Sardis. Today there is much controversy on when a person should be reckoned as medically dead. Though the church in Sardis was dead to all appearance—only the name for a short and honourable past remained—yet the Giver of life could see that a flicker of life still remained (2), and for Him that is a ground of hope.

Many of us would doubtless have told the few who were true (4) that they should come out of a dead church and be separate. However much this may have been historically necessary from time to time—in many cases the loyal ones were thrown out—there is no Scriptural justification for the proliferation of denominations in Protestantism.

Their white garments speak not merely of purity but also of life in the midst of death. For many the thought of names being blotted out of 'the book of life' (5) raises major theological difficulties. This is due to a widespread popular watering down and distortion of what may for convenience be called Calvinist teaching, though Calvin would have disowned it. It is the belief that because a person has prayed certain words, passed through certain routines, etc., he is thereby saved and saved eternally. The only proof of life is life, and the only proof of salvation is a changed life. The blotting out is presumably of that which man had assumed as certain, cf. John 20.23. The man who is content to die spiritually will not be forced by Christ to live, whatever protestations to the contrary he may have made at some time.

It should be specially noted what is said about the works of Sardis (2). Evidently in the sight of man they were admirable. It is possible for a church to get into a routine which can go on very happily even while it is dying on its feet. A great need in the Church today is for those with spiritual discernment. All too often the life of a local church is judged by pure externals, even by its numbers.

Thought: 'Every one should remain in the state in which he was called' (1 Cor. 7.20).

Revelation 3.7-13   Weak but Triumphant

The picture of 'the key of David' (7) is taken from Isa. 22.22; it speaks of Christ's kingly rule within the people of God, here the local church. The deduction from the 'open door' (8) is that there are locked ones as well. Many spend the best years of their lives battering at these and wondering why there is no clear call and blessing. Just as others cannot shut the door Christ has opened for us, so we cannot open the doors He has locked. The door, i.e. the opportunities of service, will always be proportionate to our 'power' (8)—whatever we may not be able to do, we can always keep Christ's command ('My word') and not deny His character ('My name') by our lives. For v. 9 see notes on **2.9.**

There is no point in interpreting 'the hour of trial' (10) as the great tribulation, the more so as 'the hour of testing' is the true rendering. There are recurrent judgements of God, nation-wide, even world-wide, which reveal the true nature of those who pass through them. The church in Philadelphia had already shown this, and therefore there was no need of further testing: for a similar thought, cf. 1 Pet. 4.1.

We hear too much today of crusades, campaigns and advances, and not enough of 'keep' (10), 'hold fast' (11), 'stand' (Eph. **6.13,14**). All too often more ground is lost by erosion in the church than is gained by these advances. The promise to such people, the conquerors, who have 'little power' is that they will become 'pillars' in God's temple (12). Though the promise is for the future, its reality is very often worked out in the present. The strength of the pillar is that it is rock and that it is based on rock. They are rock because the name, i.e. character, of Christ is written upon them. The features of Jerusalem's name that must be intended are 'holy' (**21.10**) and 'new'. One is holy when one belongs to and is set apart for God. Hence there is no going out. The feature implied by 'new' in Jerusalem and in Jesus' 'own new name' is a disclosure of riches and wonder only half guessed by men.

Thought: My very little becomes very much in Jesus' hands.

Revelation 3.14-22   Too Rotten to be Wicked

The last of the seven churches, Laodicea, stands lower than any of the others, even than that of Sardis. Notice that neither false doctrine nor evil living is affirmed of it. Its sin is that of Ephesus, but on a very much worse level. Ephesus had loved, and its abandoning of its first love was visible to the human eye only by comparision with what it had once been. It is doubtful whether Laodicea had fallen, for it is doubtful whether it had had anything to fall from. To the purely superficial observer it probably seemed to be what it thought itself to be (17). That is why in the introduction the unshakeable validity of Christ's judgement is stressed. As 'the prime source of all God's creation' (14, NEB) 'all things were created through Him and

50

for Him' (Col. **1**.16, cf. Col. **1**.17 f.), and so He can judge both action and motive accurately.

Both love and hatred make us very sensitive to the views of others; self-satisfaction and lukewarmness lead us to ignore their judgements. The easiest way with such people is to leave them 'to stew in their own juice', but love will reprove, and where possible deflate (19). There are few things more painful than to be entertained out of a sense of duty, so we have the picture of the Lord waiting outside the life of the lukewarm believer (20). Though we are entirely justified in using this verse in appealing to those who have no living knowledge of Christ, we should never forget that it was first said to those who claimed to be Christians. If we shut our eyes and ears to the fact that there are many Christians who have no personal experience of Christ, we only deceive ourselves. God never accepts divided loyalty, and this lukewarmness is the result of it. True fellowship in this life must involve conquering, because we cannot involve Christ in our defeats; they are evidence of the lack of His presence. Conquest means quite simply that the fellowship begun in this life is continued in eternity (21). The one difference is that at this time He transforms the humble life and home I can offer Him into His palace; then He will welcome me to His palace as one who will rule with Him, cf. 20.4,6.

Thought: The cure for lukewarmness is to ask Christ to share every department of our life.

Questions for further study and discussion on Revelation chs. 1–3

1. Note down what is said in **1**.5–8 concerning (*i*) the Person of Christ and (*ii*) the Work of Christ. To what extent does this serve as a guide for Christian preaching and teaching concerning our Lord today?
2. Since John was writing to a local congregation, try to relate his message in **2**.1–7 to your own local church.
3. 'I know your tribulation' (**2**.9). Note down facts concerning the persecution of Christians around the world of which you are aware and collect additional information from Christian papers and societies. What positive results can come from this exercise?
4. The loyal Christians in Sardis (**3**.1–6) were told to 'strengthen what remains'. How would you go about this if you were in such a church? Why were they not commanded to separate from it?

5. If reading 3.14–22 has pointed to the need for revival in your own church, what are the priorities which should occupy its members, beginning at yourself?

Revelation 4.1-8   The Throne of God

It is reasonably certain that the vision of God on His throne introduces us to a new chapter of His activity upon earth, but our identification of that moment in time will not help us to understand the vision better. The once widely held view that 'Come up hither' (1) refers to the Rapture of the Church (1 Thess. 4.16 f.) is based on an inferior text in 5.10, where the AV(KJV) has the first person, but RSV, correctly, the third.

'A throne' (2) is the symbol of rule, cf. Isa. 6.1. No more than in Isa. 6 or Ezek. 1.26 f. is there any attempt to describe God. The transparency (3) symbolizes inner purity. Perfection is indicated by the complete rainbow of one colour, contrasted with the part rainbow with broken colours we see on earth. 'The twenty-four elders' (4) are high angelic rulers; we meet this number elsewhere, e.g. 21.12–14, so they may be the guardians of the true Israel and the Church. For the 'lightning, voices, thunder' (5), cf. Exod. 20.18; Heb. 12.18 ff. Grace does not abolish law but puts it in its perfect context. 'The seven spirits of God'; see note on 1.4. For 'the sea of glass' (6), cf. Ezek. 1.22, 26; Exod. 24.10; it separates the purity of heaven from the sinfulness of earth. It is completely transparent for those who look down from there to us, but us it dazzles, hiding the glory from the eyes of sinful man.

The 'four living creatures' are the four cherubim of Ezek. 1.5–10; 10.15. It is immaterial that they are somewhat differently described, for the description is symbolic, cf. Ezek. 41.18 f., where they have only two faces. They are almost certainly also the seraphim (= the burning ones) of Isa. 6.2, as is suggested by their song. They are the representatives of God's earthly creation. The importance God attaches to it—not merely to man—is shown by their being the guardians of God's throne, or, in the symbolism of the mercy seat, His throne itself. All Biblical revelation is given to man for man, so we have God's estimate of the home He made for man. If God became man on earth, how wonderful must man and man's home be; if He died for man, how fallen must man be! Therefore, lest man who

52

receives the revelation should be proud, the song of the cherubim begins with the declaration of God's holiness, His separation from sinful man.

Revelation 4.9—5.5 The Book of the Future

From v. 9 it is clear that v. 8 is only a summary of the song of the living creatures. Since what follows primarily concerns the earth and the perfect working out of God's purposes for it, the distinctive feature of their song is thanks, in contrast to the worship of the elders; they worship in admiration, the living creatures in gratitude.

As the sequel shows, the 'scroll' (1) is the book of the future. It is in God's 'right hand' to show His control over it; it is written on both sides to show that none can add to it, and it is sealed so that none can bring it to pass before the time. We do not always sufficiently realize that Jesus Christ as the righteous and victorious Man has a special place in God's purposes. It is as Man that He is man's Saviour and man's Judge (John 5.27). Equally man's future history is entrusted into His hands. So, mysteriously, God allows the working out of His purposes to be linked with men. 'God's fellow-workers' (1 Cor. 3.9, NEB) is far more than a pious phrase.

As early as Gen. **49.**9 the lion is associated with the tribe of Judah, and traditionally the tribe used the lion on its standard. So when the Conqueror is called 'the Lion of the tribe of Judah' (5), more than a contrast with the following 'Lamb' (6) is intended. He is the fulfilment of the prophecy of Gen. **49.**9 in a higher sense than Jacob can have foreseen. 'The Root of David': cf. **22.**16, where its meaning is made clear; it is probably based on Isa. **11.**10, quoted in Rom. **15.**12. David was considered to be the great glory of Judah, with the Messiah no more than a second David. John affirms that not only is Jesus greater than His ancestor David, but that David's greatness was entirely due to the will, planning, and strength of his 'Son', whom he yet called 'Lord' (Mark **12.**35–37).

Thought: If Jesus' victory is so great that He is the Controller of the future, cannot we trust Him to control our lives in the present?

The RSV, following the AV(KJV), has sadly missed the force of v. 6. The Lamb was 'in the very middle of the throne' (NEB, Phillips). He was not 'among the elders' but in the middle of the circle formed by them and the living creatures (NEB). In other words, He occupied the central position even before He took the scroll. 'With the marks of slaughter upon him' (NEB) is preferable to 'as though it had been slain', for it makes it clearer that sacrificial death is meant. The lexicons give no support to the sentimental tradition, that we should translate 'little lamb'. The horn is a symbol of strength. In **12.3** and **13.1** the number of horns is linked with Dan. **7.7** and must be interpreted in the light of it. Here the number is clearly symbolic, the perfect number representing perfect strength, just as the 'seven eyes' show perfect knowledge.

'The prayers of God's people' (8, NEB) have such an inherent value, since they are a testimony to God's salvation and power, that they can make the worship of heaven even sweeter. Men admire ability and force; the operative word in heaven is 'worthy' (9,12).

In the dominant Greek philosophical thought of John's day matter was not merely inferior to spirit but was positively a limitation on it, and therefore evil. O.T. thought is radically opposed to this throughout. As soon as the Hebrew Christian was squeezed out of the Church, and the O.T. was increasingly neglected, Christian theology was poisoned by this Greek concept. This earth was regarded as evil and destined to be destroyed once its purpose as a testing ground for man was accomplished. The true Biblical concept was retained mainly by those regarded as sectarians or ignorant. We are told in Gen. **1.31** that God saw all that He had made was very good. This creation has been in measure marred by human sin, but to assume that this means its destruction is to affirm God's defeat, at least in one sphere. Hence in the worship of the Lamb we find the creation anticipating its deliverance (13, cf. Rom. **8.19–22**). So, too, the elders see the goal of redemption in 'they shall reign on earth' (10). This is equivalent to affirming that man will reach the original purpose of his creation, viz. having dominion (Gen. **1.26,28**). We shall see this thought taken up again at the end of the book, which ends on earth and not in heaven, or which brings heaven down to earth rather than earth up to heaven.

There are three basic principles in this section which must be grasped. (*i*) All four riders are essentially evil. Yet all four had been written beforehand in the scroll by God. The suffering of the world is not evidence of an imperfect control by God, or even of an imperfect witness by the Church. (*ii*) Nothing happens until the Lamb breaks the seals one by one. The development of human history is in the hand of Christ, and it is all working towards a predetermined end. (*iii*) It is the living creatures, the cherubim, who call on the riders to appear. Though the outcome is suffering for the creation they represent, they welcome it because it means the approach of final deliverance for the world.

Whether or not a closer historical interpretation can be given to the four riders, it is clear that they primarily represent the four main aspects of war. War is the supreme evidence for the fallen state and inner depravity of man, and so writers constantly try to justify and glamorize it more than most other evils. Its roots lie in covetousness, in the desire to possess that which belongs to others, and often in the instinct of self-preservation rooted in lack of trust in God. It always issues in theft on a grand scale with murder as its climax.

Traditionally the first rider is very often interpreted as being Jesus Christ issuing forth on His conquest of the world by the preaching of the gospel. The mention of the bow, which is never used elsewhere as a Christian symbol, should have been a sufficient warning. In addition, symbolism has an inner cohesion, which is denied when we suggest that the rider is Christ at the moment when as Lamb He is opening the seals.

Part of the attraction of war is the repeated belief that an opportunity exists for an almost bloodless victory march. Very often those who yield to this temptation find that they succeed, and the world justifies them, for they seem to guarantee peace over a wide area. In fact, sooner or later, they cause only the bitterer hostilities, which are represented by the second rider. After bloodshed and pillage there follow shortage, rationing and hunger. Then it is only a short step to famine, plague and death, and the inrush of wild animals, over which man should rule.

It is often very difficult to establish causal connections, to be sure which is cause and which effect, or whether both alike are evidence of the depravity of the human heart. It is a fact of experience, however, that the breakdown of society, linked with war and the persecution of God's people, go hand in hand. So after we have seen the horrors of war we are introduced to the sufferings of the saints.

Many interpretations of 'the altar' (9) have been offered. It could be the golden altar of incense, which is not specifically mentioned until 8.3, but this does not explain why the souls of the martyrs are under it—note that the same word, 'slain', is used for the Lamb in 5.6, cf. also John 16.2. It is probably better to understand it as the earth, which has been sanctified to God by the blood of the martyrs from Abel onwards. The abode of the dead is always pictured as under the earth. It is often said that the Second Coming is delayed so that the total number of the elect may be gathered into the Church. Here (11) the delay is so that the total of the martyrs may be complete! The 'white robe' is a guarantee of the verdict, when they stand before Christ's judgement seat, cf. 2 Tim. 4.8. It would be dangerous to draw conclusions from this passage about the amount the righteous dead know, but it certainly affirms their consciousness, as against those who teach 'soul sleep', and that they are not yet in heaven, even if the altar mentioned is there.

The language of vs. 12-14 was a commonplace in apocalyptic and eschatological literature. If we realize this, it will keep us from attributing scientifically impossible meanings to it. In general the pictures speak of the collapse and vanishing of all that seems fixed and stable in life. Nothing human can endure, if the 'earthquake' is sufficiently strong; the 'sun' and 'moon' not merely give light but also fix the seasons (Gen. 1.14-18). The 'stars' speak of God's sustaining role (Isa. 40.26, Psa. 147.4), and their vanishing is linked with the rolling up of the sky in Isa. 34.4. Just as the 'island' (14) seems to provide fixity in the midst of the stormy seas, so the 'mountain' seems to be the most stable element in a changing landscape, cf. Pss. 46.2; 121.1; Isa. 54.10; Jer. 4.24. The 'great men' (15-17) recognize the disasters for what they are, for by that time the gospel has been preached to all nations (Matt. 24.14).

· ·

Though most expositors who take this book seriously will regard this chapter as indubitably future, there are spiritual principles in it which are applicable to all times.

Dan. 7.2 explains v. 1. Long before Abraham the term 'the four corners of the earth' was used to imply universality. The 'sea' is the lawless chaos of the nations, the 'earth' is according to context either Palestine or the lands where God's law is respected, cf. 12.16, and the 'trees' the rulers and leaders. The 'winds' represent unrest and war. Repeatedly in Scripture we find a gap between the pronouncement of judgement and its fulfilment, between disaster as a warning and disaster as final. So it is here, but it is made clear (3) that the delay is less to give those who have had their warning time to repent and more to prepare those of the saints who are to pass through the intensified judgements to come. This preparation is not one of learning how to adopt a protective colouring, but the making obvious of their faith. The seal on their foreheads is where it cannot be hidden. Both seal and the sealed are apparently explained in 14.1.

In *Revelation* the distinction between true Israel and the victorious Church is reduced to a minimum (see note on 4.4). So there is little point in arguing how the Israelite tribes are to be understood. We should probably interpret in the light of 14.1. Of importance is that all God's chosen are represented, in full number, .twelve, and in ample number, 12,000. The symbolic number does not suggest that each group must of necessity be equal.

Great play has sometimes been made with the fact that Dan is apparently not included. This is one of the pieces of 'evidence' adduced for the baseless theory that the Antichrist is to come from the tribe of Dan. In fact, it is strange that along with 'Joseph' (8) 'Manasseh' also (6) is mentioned and that apparently in an unnatural position. Dan and Naphtali are generally coupled together, so it is probable that in an early manuscript Dan was read as Man, which was then interpreted as an abbreviation for Manasseh.

Thought: God's choice is perfect and its fulfilment is perfect.

In the earlier part of this chapter we saw the people of God at a given moment, and its number seemed terribly small. But when it is seen as a whole, it is 'a great multitude which no man could number' (9). There is no suggestion here that God's sealing is a guarantee of physical protection. Because the Church is the body of Christ here on earth, it has the privilege of sharing in His sufferings, cf. Col. 1.24; 2 Tim. 3.12. Whatever the details of Christ's Second Coming and the relation of the Rapture to it (1 Thess. 4.17), it is a sad fact that for very many the main stress has been laid on the 'fact' that the believer is not to pass through the great tribulation. For some, at any rate, this stress has led to a shrinking from suffering and the regarding of persecution, when it has come, as a strange thing. The sad fruits of this attitude can easily be met both at home and in many part of the mission field.

The redeemed are apparently pictured as standing even nearer the throne than the elders and the living creatures. The 'white robes' (9) are the victor's dress, but it is due to Christ's death that they are white. The 'palm branch' takes the place of the olive or laurel crown of the winner in the Greek games, the change being almost certainly to link them with John 12.13, to show that their victory was through Jesus and by the same path as His. Their position is as it should be, for where Christ is, there His people should be, too. The worship of v. 12 throws light on Eph. 3.10, for 'principalities and powers' need be understood in a bad sense only where the context demands it. The wisdom, power and love of God are specially displayed by the triumph of the Church by His grace in the midst of tribulation.

The 'elder' (13) can teach us a lesson in communication; he knew that John did not know, but he did not force the information on him. By his question he gave John the possibility of asking—'Sir, you know' (14) is a polite question—and ensured his participation. With v. 15, cf. 22.3 f. and the notes on the passage. We have the redeemed here as God's kingdom, under His protection, and His priests (cf. 1.6). There is an obvious reference to Psa. 23 in vs. 16,17. All that man experiences of God's grace on earth is only a foretaste of heaven.

Thought: Our triumph on earth can call out the highest praise of God in heaven.

Questions for further study and discussion on Revelation chs. 4–7

1. What are common concepts about God? Compare these with **4.8,11**. What needs to be emphasized concerning Him in the Church and in contemporary society?
2. Compare the qualities of the 'Lion' and the 'Lamb' as they find expression in the life of Christ.
3. Consider the statement 'The martyrs cry for vengeance (**6.9–11**)—not from personal spite, but as with the psalmist, that the honour of God may be vindicated'. Should this attitude be reflected in our lives? Does this conflict with Christlike compassion?
4. What place should the wrath of God occupy in our proclamation of the Christian faith? With the aid of a concordance note the frequency with which this concept recurs in Scripture.

Revelation 8.1-6   The Lamb's Work is Finished

Today there is a growing agreement that chs. **4–20** should be divided into a number of approximately parallel sections (**4.1–8.1**; **8.2–11.19**; **12.1–14.20**; **15.1–16.21**; **17.1–19.21**). They start at varying points but all terminate at the point of Christ's return. If that is so, **8.1** is the end of the section that began with **4.1**. When the seventh seal is broken, the silence shows that there is nothing more in the scroll. The glorified and victorious Church has echoed the 'It is finished' of its Lord. Nothing remains but for the Lamb to take up His power upon earth. Even so He can wait; the Lord knows no haste in the fulfilment of His purposes.

With v. 2 we go back in time, probably to the fifth seal (**6.9**) and see the judgements of God in more detail. As was mentioned on **6.9**, the golden 'altar' (3) is a new feature. Heb. **9.3** f. tell us that it belonged to the Holy of Holies, i.e. this is a mere shadow of the heavenly reality. Incense has a double meaning. It is that which goes up, and so it can represent prayer (**5.8**), but it also hides (Lev. **16.12** f.). So here it is that which hides God from man (Isa. **6.4**, 'smoke'), symbolized by the veil of the Tabernacle. This is a warning against taking symbolism as a sort of mathematical game in which, for the solver, two terms are interchangeable. If it were so, it would be no more than a poetic device. The seven trumpets speak primarily of God's wrath on men from whom He is hidden.

In favour of a link with **6.9** f. is the fact that the censer used for the offering of the prayers and incense is now used for the hurling of fire on the earth, prophetic of the woes to come. The fulfilment of the prayers of the martyred saints might seem a long time coming, but it was sure.

Thought: Among the virtues we must learn is patience. More harm is done through haste than slowness.

Revelation 8.7-13

God Turns the Wisdom of the Wise to Folly

The essentially symbolic nature of the woes announced is seen most clearly in v. 12. A disaster to sun and moon would decrease the total quantity of light given or reflected by them. What it could not do would be to cause darkness for a third of the night and day. Phillips' rendering shows his awareness of this, but its legitimacy may be questioned. In fact one third, and similar proportions, are a regular feature of such prophecies, cf. Zech. 13.8 f.; Ezek. 5.2,12. Major, but not irreparable disaster is indicated. At the first God's judgements are intended to be educative. It is only when they are ignored that they finally overwhelm mankind in disaster.

The reading 'eagle' (13) is justified not merely by very strong manuscript support, but also by the impossibility of explaining its presence, if 'angel', as in the AV(KJV), had been original. It must symbolize war, and the sequel in ch. 9 supports this. That being so, we may infer that the sufferings under the first three trumpets were from natural catastrophes. The fourth probably represents the trouble caused by the failure of the leaders when faced with these things. Such persons repeatedly seek to justify themselves by turning to war, in the hope that the people will forget their failures, when faced with greater perils.

There is an undue willingness in certain circles to see in any disastrous natural phenomenon a sign of the near coming of Christ. It would be far better, if we were to stress that they show most effectively the hollowness of man's claim to dominate nature. In many cases, as in China a few years ago, they are in addition clearly a Divine answer to the claim that man has everything under control, and so he does not need God, even if He exists. Politicians, who believe that they are masters in their own house and have no need of Divine guidance and help, find these visitations of nature especially galling. They cannot humble themselves to confess that there are forces completely outside their control.

Thought: 'If God wills' is not a pious formula, but a serious statement of fact. He has all the forces of nature at His command to stop us, if He wishes to.

Revelation 9.1-12 An Invasion of Demons

Efforts to identify the scourge here described with some known nation past or present have carried little conviction, but an application of symbolism may help us. The 'star fallen from heaven' (1) will be as symbolic as in 8.12; in the light of 12.9, Luke 10.18, it may well be Satan that is meant. He does not possess the key of 'the shaft of the abyss' (NEB)—the rendering 'bottomless pit' is justified neither by the Greek nor by common sense—it is given him, obviously by the Lamb. However much Satan may wish to wreck God's work, he is the agent of His will, cf. Job 1,2.

Those that rise from the abyss are obviously demons, but the demon has seldom, if ever, power over nature as such—they are not to harm the grass or trees (4)—but over evil men whom they enter and control. Hence they cannot hurt those with God's seal. The predominant impression they create is of the beast—'horses' (7)—for the demon-possessed is always essentially sub-human, even where this is not immediately clear. He claims to rise above human limitations, hence the 'crown' (7). The reference to 'women's hair' (8) may be to remind us that the inrush of evil is almost always linked with an apparent glorification of sex, which always leads to its debasement. They are pictured as an army. There are many periods when evil puts on the mask of goodness, even as Satan may appear as an angel of light, but there are others, and we are passing through one now, when evil is in embattled opposition to God. We find ourselves in the position of Eph. 6.10–18, when we may be thankful, if we have been able to do no more than stand our ground. 'Abaddon', cf. Job 26.6; 28.22; 31.12; Psa. 88.11; Prov. 15.11; 27.20, means, like 'Apollyon', destruction, and is another name for death or Sheol. Demon influence tortures man first of all, and in the end destroys him.

Of special importance is the mention of 'five months' (5,10). This is the first of numerous passages where a fixed number is mentioned. It is not the interpretation of the period that is important, but that we realize that the apparent triumph of evil is God-permitted and controlled, its very beginning and ending being fixed in advance.

Revelation 9.13-21 Evil Let Loose

The forces in this section are as clearly demonic as in the previous one, though probably physical as well as spiritual warfare is intended. Here again there is an exact indication of time given, in this case of when the disaster is to break out (15). Its duration is governed by the time taken to accomplish their task. It should be noted that, because the evil done seems to be physical rather than spiritual, there is no mention of God's people being spared, cf. v. 4.

No explanation is given as to who 'the four angels' (14) may be; that they are bound suggests that they are fallen ones; that they are four—see note on 7.1—may imply that they represent the fallen angels as a whole, and they may be the otherwise unexplained 'cavalry' (16). The Euphrates (14) seems to play a symbolic part in Biblical thinking. It served as a kind of symbolic frontier between civilization and barbarism. Civilization, in Johannine language, the world, is on the one hand a gift of God (Rom. 13.1), on the other it has been twisted by Satan and evil men into an obstacle to the advance of God's will and rule. So God has repeatedly allowed the stable world to be rocked to its foundations by the inrush of barbarism. Sometimes it has been like a tidal wave of barbarian destruction, which in due course has ebbed again. Sometimes their way has been prepared by propaganda, as with the inrush of Communism, which has often effectively destroyed all desire to resist. It should not be forgotten that the totalitarian systems of our day are essentially a perverted Communism, a seeking to use Satan to drive out sin. We should be staggered, could we reckon how many lives have been lost through Communism, Nazism and Fascism of various kinds.

Whenever such judgements have come, the result has always been the same. Men have never turned as a body from the worship of their false gods, and from their crimes, whether they are crude ones like those mentioned in vs. 20 f. or the rather more subtle ones of today. If anything, disaster is explained away by saying that the worship of these gods had not been thorough enough. 'Sorceries' (21) is probably not a satisfactory rendering; it probably refers to drug traffic, either to murder or to create willingness to sin.

Revelation 10.1-11 The Mystery of God Draws to an End

It is generally agreed that there are two visions (**10**.1–11; **11**.1–13) which form a parenthesis before the blowing of the seventh trumpet in **11**.15. So far as the former is concerned, there is no evidence that it should be fitted into the developing revelation, however this is understood. It is rather a message to the seer, returned for a moment to earth—the angel came down (1)—for if we respond to revelation we may expect more to be given us.

The identity of the 'angel' (1) is immaterial. The various attributes, like cloud, rainbow, sun, are not to identify him with Christ, but are to make it clear that he is speaking with the authority of God. The 'little scroll' (2) is not that of **5**.1, but looks back to Ezek. **2**.9–**3**.3, and is John's continuing message. It is smaller, because no man in his personal ministry can hope to do justice to every aspect of God's revelation. The message concerned the people of God ('the land') and the nations at large ('the sea'). 'The seven thunders' (3) did not merely sound, they spoke (NEB). No indication of their nature or of what they said is given. They may have given revelation beyond what John had to reveal; we must confine ourselves to what God teaches us. On the other hand it may have been the opposition of apparently authoritative circles. We are not to record and so give longer life to voices that oppose God's revelation.

The rendering of the AV(KJV) and RV text in v. 6 ('there shall be time no longer') is unfortunate; it has given rise to unprofitable theories about the timelessness of eternity and its consequent stagnation. God's 'mystery' (7), or 'hidden purpose' (NEB), has been revealed, but our full understanding of it awaits the end of present history. The subtle difference between v. 10 and Ezek. **3**.3 should be noted. There is a bitter element in the gospel which cannot be eliminated without distorting it. It is a fragrance from death to death among those who are perishing (2 Cor. **2**.15 f.). At the age he had reached, relaxation from his labours would have seemed natural for John. There is no doubt, however, that his Gospel and letters were written after this. Though John is called the apostle of love, he has some of the sternest and straightest language in the Bible about lovelessness and sin.

Thought: When God teaches us, it is that we may teach others.

There is no part of *Revelation* which has lent itself more to fanciful interpretations than this, but we shall ignore them. No description of the measuring is given. It was doubtless performed in vision, for it seems to be a temple on earth, and that in Jerusalem had already been destroyed by Titus. The measuring is doubtless of the same nature as the sealing in 7.3, i.e. the guaranteeing of God's care, and the temple is God's people, cf. Eph. 2.19-22; 2 Cor. 6.16; once again there is no need to distinguish between the Church and the true Israel. There are no grounds for identifying it with the temple of 11.19. 'The court outside' (2), the court of the Gentiles, represents all that mixed multitude which at most times is associated with the people of God, cf. Isa. 1.12. For the 'forty-two months' in v. 2, cf. 11.3; 12.6,14; 13.5; it is the same period as that in Dan. 7.25; 12.7. We need not doubt that there will be a fulfilment in a later day, when the time will be literally fulfilled, but it is also symbolic, for it represents half the great week of God's purposes, nor may we forget that in Dan. 9.24 we are dealing with a day equalling a year. So long God can allow His adversaries to have their way.

The 'two witnesses' (3) are linked through v. 4 with Zech. 4, where they are Zerubbabel and Joshua. Without our ruling out the possibility of literal fulfilment, we should recognize that they speak to us of due leadership within the people of God, who maintain its witness. The triumph of the beast (7) links with 13.7, where it is imperative that a wide meaning be found. We should note the short period of the beast's triumph compared to the length of the witness.

The same movement within a narrower and wider meaning is seen in the description of the city (8). While in its narrower sense it refers to Jerusalem, the description 'great city' asks us to look outwards. Jerusalem is compared with Sodom in Isa. 1.10; Ezek. 16.46-56, but never with Egypt. What is true of apostate Jerusalem is true of apostate civilization generally. The disciples understood this, cf. Acts 4.25-27.

Question: Are you willing to be defeated for Jesus' sake?

Revelation 11.15-19   Christ is King!

We now reach the same point as 8.1. The apparent difference and even contradiction is due to the nature of symbolism. A symbol never claims to represent more than one aspect of the truth. Therefore two symbols may be used for the same event, which at first sight are incompatible. Silence (8.1) brought out the completion of Christ's work in the Church. Here we have the response of the heavenly powers to it.

'The kingdom of the world' (15): very much better is 'the sovereignty of the world' (NEB) or 'the kingship of the world' (Phillips); see note on 1.6. God has always ruled the world, but the majority of men have been in revolt against Him. Since God willed to control the animal creation through man (Gen. 1.26–28; Psa. 8.5–8; Heb. 2.5–9), man's revolt and fall mean that God's rule in the animal world is only partially discernible. At this point we see Phil. 2.10 f. about to go into effect.

If we are to understand the frequent prosperity and well-being of the wicked—there are many exceptions; while Stalin died in his bed as an old man, Mussolini died by violence and Hitler by his own hand—we must grasp that the sufferings of this present time are seldom God's punishment, which awaits the final judgement. They are partly the sequel of broken law, but even more God's effort to bring man to his senses. The sufferings that precede the coming of Christ, 'the birth pangs of the Messiah' (Mark 13.8), which have been repeatedly foreshadowed in history, are intended to break man's will to resist, even though they do not necessarily bring him to faith.

'Thy wrath' (18): God's wrath is essentially 'the wrath to come' (1 Thess. 1.10, cf. 1 Thess. 5.9; Matt. 3.7); that is why the NEB renders very well, 'Thy day of retribution'. It is revealed in man's sufferings and above all in his being 'given up' (Rom. 1.24,26,28), but all this is only a foretaste of that to come, which finds its climax in the seven plagues (15.1). We should avoid replacing wrath by anger. There is normally an element of reaction to the wrong done to oneself in anger; in God's wrath there is merely the reaction to the wrong done to others. The climax of God's judgement is on 'the destroyers of the earth' (18).

For the temple in heaven (19), cf. 15.5. Presumably we are to infer that the earthly Tabernacle and Temple are merely symbols of the heavenly reality seen in ch.4.

Questions for further study and discussion on Revelation chs. 8–11

1. Does God use disasters to punish men? Have they any other function? Note the disasters of the O.T.: earthquake (*Amos*), famine (*Amos*), foreign powers (Isa.10), locusts and drought (*Joel*).

2. The new age in which we now live has changed the status of Satan. How far? Examine his activities, not only in the light of *Revelation*, but in the rest of the N.T.
3. What were the bitter-sweet results of the Word of God in the experience of John and, more particularly, in the life of Paul? Is it possible to have one without the other?
4. Have we any way of knowing today whether the end is near?
5. Why must imagery and metaphor be used to describe spiritual realities?

Revelation 12.1-6 Satan and the People of God

Again a new section begins; 'And' (1) is only the introduction common in Hebrew narrative. The measure of time (6) puts it before 11.3, but more we cannot say. Few passages of Scripture have given rise to more diverse interpretations, so the following must be regarded merely as an effort to take the symbolism seriously.

The section 12.1–14.5 is played out on three levels: the throne of God (Mount Zion), heaven, and earth; they are to be understood of spiritual status, not of physical position, cf. Eph. 2.6. The sun, moon and stars link the woman with Israel (Gen. 37.9), to be understood, as elsewhere in *Revelation*, as the people of God. The 'red dragon' (3) is identified with the devil (9). It is red because Satan is a murderer from the beginning (John 8.44). The heads and horns are identical with those of the second beast (13.1); it is easier to explain them in the latter (see notes), so we may assume that Satan is thus pictured in order to show that the second beast is a real reproduction on earth of Satan and his system. If in the former the diadems are on the heads, in the latter on the horns, it shows that the sovereignty is only delegated in the second. In v. 4 we have an intensification of Dan. 8.10; here it probably refers to the seducing of many of the angelic host.

What of the 'male child' (5)? The apparently obvious meaning is Jesus, but why should there be a reference back to His birth? In addition, v. 5 would be a strange summary of His earthly work. Chapters 2.26 f.; 20.4 suggest that he personifies the conquerors, the true Church within the Church that claims the name, cf. 14.1–5; Eph. 5.27.

The woman is seen in heaven and on earth, i.e. the 'wilderness' (6). This is the contrast between the people of God as seen by God, and in their humiliation as seen by man, as they are judged by God and man to be. When they are most despised by man, they are most in the place prepared by God for them, and where they will find God's provision.

Revelation 12.7-12   The Defeat of Satan

Popular Christian fantasy, basing itself on this passage, Isa. 14.12, etc., has pictured a war in which God's angels led by Michael threw Satan and his angels out of heaven long before the creation of man. There is no Scriptural warrant for this, least of all in this passage.

What is described is something within the range of events described by *Revelation* and affecting its readers (12). What is more, the defeat of Satan is merely symbolic, for the victory has been won by the conquerors within the Church (11), thus almost certainly confirming the interpretation given to the male child (5). Whether or not this scene has a yet future application and climax, it has worked itself out throughout the history of the Church. They had conquered Godwards by their trust in Christ's death, and manwards by their witness. Because in both directions they had renounced trust in what they did themselves, 'they loved not their lives even unto death' (11). This must not be understood merely as a willingness to embrace a martyr's death, but also as a renunciation of success as the world inside and outside the Church esteems it.

By their victory they first of all shut the mouth of Satan (= the Accuser). As the image of Christ was formed in them, cf. 2 Cor. 3.18, they demonstrated to the world that Satan is not its ruler and that there is a greater power than his, thus depriving him of his place in man's esteem. Doubtless there will be a great, final demonstration of this, but it is something that has had to be worked out again in each new generation. The Church is never in greater danger than when it is acclaimed by the world, for it may allow itself to be persuaded that there is some merit in it, and that there is something it can achieve. When the Church allows its task and methods to be dictated by the world, it is the subtle recognition of the wisdom of Satan, prince of this world.

Perhaps the most important lesson of this section is that we must not look on the Church merely as the sphere of salvation, but as that of God's continuing victory in Christ. The body of Christ is no mere empty metaphor but a living reality, cf. Eph. 1.22 f. (NEB); 3.10; Col. 1.24.

We have to distinguish between the willingness to suffer martyrdom (11) and the foolhardy challenging of death. Jesus Himself commanded His disciples to flee to another city when they were persecuted (Matt. 10.23), implying that the message would be better spread that way. Here (14) we see the people of God going underground for the time being, something that has been more frequent and more fruitful than is often realized. The wings symbolize the speed at which it happens. There is always a danger, when the Church becomes too anchored and hampered by physical things which restrict its mobility.

The symbolism in vs. 15,16 is probably clear in general outline but difficult to apply in detail. The earth always stands symbolically for that which is firm and steadfast, and hence law-abiding. Sometimes, but hardly here, it represents Israel as the people under God's law. The water-floods, whether the sea, or as here a river in spate, represent the nations in their lawlessness and rebellion against God. So the picture is of Satan loosing mob violence against the Church, as he has so often done. Indeed, in every age State action against the Church has often been based on popular demand. Here, however, the forces of law and order react against the mob violence and foil it. But as ch. 13 shows us, this merely means that subtlety is substituted for force by the enemy.

Satan changes his attack from the Church as such to its members. The description of them (17) precludes any interpretation that they are those left behind at the Rapture. They are surely the male child unrecognized in their humble state.

Thought: Keeping the commandments of God and witnessing go together.

In Dan. 7.3 four beasts come out of the sea. Here there is only one (1), but it combines the traits of the first three (2, cf. Dan. 7.4–6), and as it develops, it shows another trait, its mouth, which links it with the fourth (5, Dan. 7.8,20); this is in any case shown by its horns (1, Dan. 7.7). As Dan. 7.17 makes clear, the beast is both a man and a system. It is in fact the summing up of an age-old system, which John calls the world, and of a line of men who have sought to rule in defiance of God's will. Its last stage is merely the climax of what has been all along. It comes out of the sea (1), i.e. it is the product of mankind in rebellion against God; it is a beast, because man in revolt against God is sub-human. Even the mortally wounded head (3) is only a special case of a common phenomenon. Repeatedly in human history a system or ruler is saved when at the apparent point of death. This is regarded as proof of divine favour, and honour and validity are attributed which are in fact a worship of Satan.

Far more effective than mob violence against the believer is to embrace him in the omnicompetent, authoritarian State, which may give lip-service to God, but by its claims it blasphemes Him. The dragon may give the beast his power (2), but only God can allow it to make war on the saints and conquer them (7), and doubtless it is also God who gives it its authority (cf. Rom. 13.1), though its length is strictly limited (5). From v. 7 we see that these principles are world-wide.

In thê Holy Communion we take the bread as symbol of Christ's body of humiliation, not of His glorified body. Similarly the Church follows in the steps of His humiliation, even though it may enjoy hours of popular favour, as He did. Periodically, not only in the end time, the Church knows the bitterness of apparent defeat and death. Only so can God separate the true from the false. Natural man's sights are set on the present or immediate future, the spiritual man's on the end of the age, when Christ returns and true judgement is meted out (10), cf. 14.16–20.

Question: Do you expect more from life than Jesus did, cf. Matt. 10.24,25?

Revelation 13.11-18 The Mark of the Beast

The very fact that the second beast rises out of 'the earth' (11) suggests its nature. It represents every organization that claims to accept God's law, but is opposed to its spirit. Very much ingenuity has been used in interpreting the number of the beast (18), and some of the interpretations may have a limited validity. But 'wisdom', and not a knowledge of Greek, or even Hebrew, is called for (18). The RSV is among the few translations that realizes that 'the number of a man' is a false translation; 'it is a human number', or the number of mankind. Seven is symbolically the perfect number, God's number; six is the number of man at his best. 666 is man at the climax of his achievement, but still falling short of the perfection of 777. The details of the vision are not so important as the realization that we have essentially the worship of man depicted, which is indirectly the worship of Satan, as lord of the world.

There are times when the killing of those who refuse to worship (15) is to be taken literally; sometimes no more than the squeezing out of the non-conformist is involved. The reference is not to ration cards, though these show how easily the vision can be carried out, but to the raising of human organizations, particularly those of the State, to complete power. There was a time, when either by the inefficiency of the State machine, or by moving to virgin lands, men could opt out. Today this has become impossible, and it is merely a question of how much authority the State chooses to exert. The fact that in almost every land liberal, not necessarily Christian, men are alarmed by the growth of State power shows how far we have gone.

Perhaps our greatest danger is the belief that we extend our influence by increasing and strengthening our Christian organizations. However pure their doctrine, they are in danger of being caught up in the orbit of the second beast. One of the saddest lessons from the Communist and Nazi dictatorships is the way in which they have been able to capture and, in great measure, use completely admirable church organizations.

Thought: One of the Christian's greatest problems is to hold in balance subjection to the authorities with a rejection of the Satanic powers that use them.

Revelation 14.1-5 The Conquerors

Though Mt. Zion is repeatedly used as a symbol for God's throne among men, it is never so used for something future, separated from this earth; see especially Heb. 12.22, which speaks of a present reality. It seems to be the symbolic expression here of Eph. 2.6. We return to the 'male child' and see what his being caught up to the throne of God really meant.

The conquering Christian lives on two planes simultaneously. One we saw in 13.7, but all the time the beast seemed to be triumphing he was in fact being conquered. The mention of the Father's name (1) is a reminder that it is possible to develop a worship of the purely earthly Jesus of Nazareth, which is as one-sided as the ignoring of His earthly life.

The literal rendering of v. 4, 'These are they who did not defile themselves with women, for they are virgins' has led to a false exaltation of celibacy. Such an understanding assumes that the whole company is male, which is never otherwise suggested, and it commits the cardinal fault in exegesis of taking a symbolic passage literally. It also assumes that marriage causes some form of defilement. Over half the instances of the word-groups of adultery and fornication (whoredom) in the O.T. are applied to the worship of other gods, or to a conception of Jehovah which He refused to recognize, and that is surely the meaning here. In this day of the overvaluing of sex, every young Christian should consider passages like Matt. **19**.10–12; 1 Cor. **7**.7,8,25,26,32–35 prayerfully, but let him not forget that under other circumstances Paul commanded marriage (1 Tim. **5**.14). Above all there is never any suggestion that celibacy increases a person's standing as a Christian; most of the apostles were married (1 Cor. **9**.5).

It should be specially noted that the evidence that they 'follow the Lamb wherever He goes' (4) is that they do not lie (5). Lies are caused by two things, fear and pride, which cause personal desires to take the chief place. Both disappear in the presence of Christ; cf. also **21**.8,27; **22**.15.

This close contact with their Lord also enables them to understand Him and the purposes of God better and more clearly. It is this that is implied by the 'new song' (3) that others could not learn. Salvation does not depend on understanding God and what He has done in this way; scholarship will not teach it and spiritual exaltation will not give it. It comes from fellowship and obedience, and the two cannot really be separated.

Revelation 14.6-13   God Has the Last Word

It is probably best to see in **14**.6–20 the climax of the vision of **12**.1– **14**.5, and its inevitable outcome. The Victorian period with its frills and furbelows, its knick-knacks and aspidistras, loved complication, and so many saw in the 'eternal gospel' (6) a special and different one for the world after the rapture of the Church. Today we are learning that God's greatness is seen above all in a simplicity too great for man to grasp. The expression of the gospel at any time takes on a special form, for it should always be adapted to the circumstances of the hearers (note the indefinite article in RSV), but essentially it is eternal and unchangeable. A preaching of the cross that neglects the eternal sovereignty of God is always less than the gospel.

Here in the face of the apparent triumph of the beast the abiding sovereignty of God is proclaimed. This is reinforced by the fall of

71

'Babylon' (8), both ecclesiastical and commercial (see notes on chs. **17,18**), which means the humbling of human pride. So then the third call is for mental and spiritual revolt against the enthralment of the beast (9), which for so long had bedazzled men. The true Christian does not and will not worship the beast. The one who has been misled and has worshipped him in ignorance is given the opportunity of repentance.

We tend to smile indulgently at the practice of keeping up with the Joneses, but we repeatedly fail to see what it hides. It puts what I have before what I am, and makes possessions the standard of judgement; it exalts the temporary above the eternal. It is the implicit rejection of all that Jesus' life meant. When such people are faced with the realities of eternity, it means torment.

The last mile of the road, the last lap of the race, the last round of the fight, is always the hardest. The clear evidence that the systems of this world are breaking down and chaos is coming in will be the most taxing for the Church. Even today so many feel that there should be rest rather than light at eventide. It will be extra hard for those who die just as they fancy they can see the light of Christ's return on the horizon. So there is a special word of encouragement for them (13).

Revelation 14.14-20 The Harvest

The great difference between Biblical religion and probably all others is its sense of final purpose. Islam and Mahayana Buddhism believe in a judgement after death, but neither sees any real purpose behind the world process. Equally, modern philosophies including Marxism and Humanism may offer motives for what is considered good behaviour, but they have no real goal for human history. For the Bible human history is surely, if very slowly, moving towards that moment when God's triumph will be obvious, not so much because He crushes opposition—if that were His purpose, He could and would have done so long ago—but because the harvest is ripe, and the difference between wheat and tares is finally obvious. His goal is that man should accept His will, and that this acceptance be seen as man's greatest good. 'One like a son of man' (14): from the context it seems improbable that Jesus Christ is meant, cf. also Matt. 13.39,41,49.

If here the contrast is between grain and grapes, it is not a disparagement of the latter, or of the wine made from them—they can be used of the fruit borne by the Christian (John **15**.2,5)—but because of the picture offered by the treading of the grapes in the wine press (**19.15**; Isa. **63.3**). 'Outside the city' (20): normally a wine press would be outside the city walls. Here, however, 'the city' is probably Jerusalem. This would link it with what is normally called the battle of Armageddon (**16.16**), though this is in fact merely mentioned as the mustering place for the army. The implications of the last battle will be dealt with when commenting on **19.11–21**. Here it is sufficient to underline that the vision deals with the results of active and deliberate opposition to God.

'The angel who has power over fire' (18): the Greek is 'the fire'. Probably lightning is meant. This was regarded in the ancient world as peculiarly the expression of God's power, and in its suddenness and devastating destruction still reminds man of his weakness and insignificance.

Question: If man chooses to fight God, why should he be saved from the consequences?

Questions for further study and discussion on Revelation chs. 12–14

1. What factors account for the persecution of Christian churches? What may be deduced from the fact that the western churches are relatively free from persecution?

2. What is involved in the statement 'They loved not their lives even unto death' (**12.11**)? Examine this in the light of the teaching of our Lord, John and Paul.

3. Chapters **12,13** say much about Satan's attack on the Church. Which methods does he employ most successfully today?

4. Examine the N.T. references to antichrist and antichrists. What are the characteristics and functions involved?

5. What rule of life is set out for Christians in **13.10**? Using a concordance see how this is stressed in the N.T.

Revelation 15.1-8   The Seven Last Plagues

In this chapter we find ourselves at the same point in the development in God's purposes as **7.9–17** and **19.1–10**. The rapture of the Church is past (**14.14** f.), and the grape harvest (**14.17–20**) is about to be reaped. We here see that the plagues are an interpretation of the treading out of the grapes. There are 'seven plagues' (1) for reasons mentioned earlier; they are the full, perfect and final pouring out of God's wrath. We shall be safe in assuming that they occupy very little time.

The 'sea of glass' (2) is that of 4.6, but where it formerly merely dazzled the earth-dweller, now, once the Church has gone, the signs of the imminent judgement ('fire') befleck it. The 'harps of God' (2): better 'the harps which God had given them' (NEB). 'The song of Moses and . . . of the Lamb' (3): as has been repeatedly said, John does not draw any clear distinction between the true Israel and the conquering Church; here both are represented, hence the double song. Yet Israel can sing the song of the Lamb, for all the time it had looked forward to His coming, even if it had not recognized Him, and the Church can sing the song of Moses, for Christ is the completion of the O.T. and of its hope (John 8.56). 'The song of Moses' refers back to Exod. 15.1–18. It matters very little whether we read 'King of the ages' (3) or 'of the nations'. The song of triumph recognizes that God has not merely guided and ruled His people, but has guided (Amos 9.7) and overruled the nations which did not accept Him, as well as the ages to which human thinkers could give no meaning.

'The temple of the tent of witness' (5): far better 'the sanctuary of the heavenly Tent of Testimony' (NEB); for the concept, cf. Heb. 8.5. The angels have, like the Lord (1.13), their breasts girded with golden girdles to show that they act as His representatives. The Tent was filled with smoke so that none could enter (8), for those on whom the plagues were to fall had made their choice, and it was too late to repent.

Thought: If you say No often enough, God will take you at your word.

Revelation 16.1-7   The First Three Plagues

Since all the plagues are future, every attempt to give a definitive explanation to the symbolism is likely to fall short. Yet here, as elsewhere in the book, we shall probably do better taking the details symbolically rather than literally.

We live in a time when most still try to keep a façade of respectability for their lives, and it is still possible for many in the public eye to hush up scandals until after their death. The minority who do not trouble about appearances nevertheless try to justify their actions by terms like freedom and self-expression, a brushing away of hypocrisy, etc. Now, however, the reality of an evil life is to be made clear to all; the inner is to become visible.

One of the results of the gospel was very gradually to teach Christendom that violence was evil, and murder a unique sin. This recognition was always superficial; with the increasing rejection of the gospel violence has become a commonplace, and we find even Christian ministers advocating the use of violence to right wrongs. Hence murder has become only one crime among many. With the removal of the Church, murder and violence become the characteristic of the nations—'the sea' (3); in O.T. thought 'the blood of a dead man' means life violently taken.

Since 'the angel of water' (5) approves of the third plague, it is clear that 'the rivers and fountains of water' (4) are something good. In Eastern Mediterranean lands water is the most important of the gifts of heaven, and, except in Egypt, it came through rain at the right time. So we should probably think of a breakdown of the great uniformities of nature (Gen. 8.22) and of God's beneficent providence (Matt. 5.45). It is a sign of human pride that so few today are any longer prepared to see the hand of God in drought and flood, storm and unseasonable weather. The picture of blood is taken from Exod. 7.17–21. Just as we can only infer the causes of the first plague in Egypt, so we must reserve judgement here; in both cases blood refers to the colour, not composition of the water. The first two plagues strike at man's pride in himself and the society he has created, the third at his vaunted domination of nature.

When we hear 'the altar cry' (7), we are fairly safe in interpreting it as of the earth as in 6.9. The O.T. concept of the involvement of the soil in the life of those that live on it has been almost completely lost today.

Thought: Man can achieve the worth-while only by God's permission.

Revelation 16.8-16 Keep Awake!

Since none of the other heavenly bodies is here mentioned with 'the sun' (8), there is no reason why we should not take it literally. A very small rise in the sun's inner temperature could raise that of the earth to an almost unbearable level beside causing major natural disasters by the melting of glaciers and the polar ice-caps. The darkness over the beast's capital (Babylon?) and the heart of his kingdom is doubtless to be explained as in Exod. 10.21. Drought and great heat—nor may we exclude the possibility of volcanic action (18,19)—create the conditions for a major sand storm. The result of these two plagues justify the grape harvest of judgement (14.17–20). The man who does not respond to God's love will not humble himself before His judgements.

For the symbolic meaning of the Euphrates see note on **9.14**. We are probably intended to see the breakdown of civilization under the inrush of the underprivileged peoples from all sides—not only the east is intended. Faced with the breakdown of all that Satanic wiles, human pride and religious self-confidence had created, the three beasts plan a supreme come-back. Since the war on the saints (**13.7**) is not to be understood literally, neither should that on God. Armageddon is named as the mustering place, not the battle ground. Since it is the largest plain in Palestine, it points to the size of the forces involved. There is no suggestion of an attack on Jerusalem; we must beware how we try to piece different prophecies into a tidy unity, as though they were bits of a jig-saw. The mustering is done by 'demonic spirits' (14), so it seems that a supreme effort is being made to get men to abjure God.

In spite of their horror, the plagues are merely intensifications of what has already happened, just as the plagues on Egypt were of natural troubles that have often stricken the land. So Christian readers are warned that the judgements of God are abroad in the land and so they must keep awake (15), cf. 1 Thess. **5.2–8**. The temple area was a fortress and Levitical troops used to be on duty at night. At an unpredictable hour the 'captain of the temple' used to make his rounds. Should he find a sentry asleep, he took a torch from one of the escort and set his clothes on fire; with morning light his burnt appearance proclaimed to all his companions his failure in his duty, cf. 1 John **2.28**.

Revelation 16.17-21 It is Done!

We have again reached the same point as **8.1**; **11.15–19**; **14.17–20**. Though there is no connection, the fear shown by so many of atomic fallout will show what the pouring of the last bowl 'into the air' (17) means. Everywhere, with no nook or cranny left for safety, the wrath of God floats down on men, leaving nothing more to be awaited. With v. 18, cf. **8.5**; if the divisions of the book suggested are correct, it is an intensification we are now dealing with, but it is one of the signs which justify us in thinking that God constantly causes man to experience foreshadowings of what is to be.

The meaning of the great city (19) was discussed in the notes on **11.8**; cf. also **17.9,18**. Though there is no reason why Jerusalem should not be included, it is most doubtful whether any exclusive reference to it is intended. The first two cities recorded in the Bible are Enoch (Gen. **4.17**) and Babel (Gen. **11.4**), and both were expressions of lack of trust in God, cf. Heb. **11.10**. What is here being proclaimed is the complete destruction of man's last line of defence against both God and chaos.

'Great Babylon' (19): though Babylon is not mentioned in Scripture between Gen. **11.9**—Babel is the Hebrew name for Bab-ili, which we render Babylon—and the days of Hezekiah, it had a position all its own in Hebrew thought. Though it had little political importance between its capture by the Kassites in 1530 B.C. and its being made the capital of a Chaldean empire in 626 B.C., it was the virtually undisputed commercial and religious capital of the Fertile Crescent. So it is the personification, so to speak, for the Bible, of man organized for financial profit, and of man-made religion in all its attractive sophistry. These are the two aspects which are dealt with in chs. **17** (religion) and **18** (commerce). If we compare *Nahum* and *Habakkuk*, we shall learn something of the different impression created by the pride and cruelty of Assyria and the corruption of human nature which the prophet saw in Babylon.

'Hailstones' (21): cf. Job **38**.22 f. For the inhabitants of the Eastern Mediterranean lands it was a supreme sign that something was wrong with the world, when the rain which was the supreme blessing could become a threat to life and property as it was turned to ice. So hail was looked on supremely as a sign of Divine intervention and anger; here it can be anything that carries that message.

Revelation 17.1-6   Babylon the Harlot

It is the religious aspect of Babylon we are here considering. She is called 'the great harlot' (1) because false religion, like false sex, cheats; it gives only a counterfeit, never the reality. She is riding 'a scarlet beast' (3), which is later clearly identified with that of **13.1**, or sitting on 'many waters' (1), rightly rendered 'the ocean' (NEB), cf. v. 15; Dan. **7.2**, i.e. the nations. Here we have religion not as a political organization, but as exercising power through the State. This involves 'the harlot' in supporting the State; that is the price she must pay for power. Since God and the world are in irreconcilable conflict, religion must adopt the world's values to retain its position. So she is seen in 'a wilderness' (3); she kills true spiritual life.

Marx, when he said, 'Religion is the opium of the people', probably did not know that he was repeating the maxim of one of the Cromwellian Levellers or Fifth Monarchy men. In its original sense it is true. Every religious system, to preserve its own existence,

77

is tempted to preach obedience to something in addition to Christ. In the measure it does this it belongs to the harlot. We may think that one system more than others is the harlot, but John makes no effort to identify her. We may also think that for someone to belong to such a system automatically taints him. Experience has shown that Christ leaves some of His choicest saints in such churches, that they may resist, often at great loss, the lust for power and the demand for obedience where it must not be given.

While it is the beast that persecutes, the impulse comes from the harlot (cf. 13.16, where the second beast is referred to that represents the religious side of persecution). The official world has normally very little fear of the saint, for it knows that he has no itch to rule, no desire to seize power. It has been only when rulers have deified themselves, like the Roman emperors, or have claimed religious power they had no right to, like some Reformation monarchs, or virtually deified the State, like modern totalitarian systems, that the secular power has persecuted in its own interests. We are told the harlot was 'drunk' (6). That is one of the worst aspects of persecution. Once it starts, it seems to know no bounds; this is as true when it is done in the name of orthodoxy as in that of false teaching.

Revelation 17.7-18   The Fate of the Harlot

John tells us that when he saw the harlot, 'I was greatly astonished' (6, NEB). If it were not that we are so familiar with the existence and history of the official Church, we should probably be so, too. At the time the Roman Empire was turning itself into a god; it was uninterested in religious systems unless they claimed first place, and then it persecuted them. So in that sense the beast 'is not' (8). From the time of Constantine the new alliance began. Wherever European civilization has become dominant, in one way or another the story has repeated itself. Even in the United States, where established religion is barred by the constitution, the Christian churches enjoy much privilege.

Though Rome is not the only city to have been built on seven hills—the same is asserted of Jerusalem—there can be no doubt that it looms large in the picture, and we need not be surprised that for the Reformers the identification of the harlot with the Roman Catholic Church was almost an article of faith. This is the more natural, if we remember that Constantinople (as later Moscow) had claimed to be the heir of Rome. In so symbolic a book we may, however, question an interpretation that may deflect attention from one's own denomination. We have met seven before, and the hills are the symbol of stability. At all times the established church has been the chief supporter of the establishment. The identification of the harlot with organized society is seen in her being called 'the great city' (18).

There is a tendency in some circles to link certain modern church groupings with the harlot. All church groupings that aim at or exercise power fall into her orbit. So do the organizations set up to fight them. Every church organization seeking power and setting its own claims for loyalty has been so drawn.

In the end the beast tires of the harlot and destroys her. This is a process that began with the French Revolution, if not earlier. It has been greatly advanced by the rise of Marxism and totalitarianism. Already politicians have little time for the pronouncements of Church circles. The final overthrow of the harlot, when the world will appear unmasked as unashamedly anti-God, will show that the end is very near.

Questions for further study and discussion on Revelation chs. 15–17

1. Compare the Song of Moses (Exod. 15) with 15.3 f. What connection is there between these two songs? What concepts concerning God are emphasized? Do they figure prominently in our worship?

2. Note the recurring phrase 'they did not repent' (ch. 16). Why do people react to disaster in this way?

3. Have the judgements of God been neglected in contemporary preaching? If so, how can this be rectified without negating the fact of His love?

4. What concept of God has the modern man? How would you seek to present a balanced N.T. picture of God to the non-Christian? Where would you start and how would you proceed?

5. What is blasphemy?

Revelation 18.1-8   Babylon the Great

How inextricably the harlot church and human society are intertwined is shown by the difficulty in realizing that we have moved to another Babylon. The passage is shot through with memories of the prophets, e.g. Isa. 13.21; 14.23; 34.11,13; Jer. 50.39; 51.37 for v. 2, and Jer. 50.15; 51.9; Isa. 47.7,8; Zeph. 2.13 for vs. 6,7.

The call to come out of her, which shows that in v. 1 we have the 'prophetic perfect', i.e. that which is about to happen is spoken of as though it has already occurred, is parallel to 2 Cor. 6.14–18, which is quoted from Isa. 52.11. It is to be noted that in none of the three cases is there any question of leaving some form of corrupt Christianity, whether doctrine or life is involved. Here it refers to the money-based commercial power-system that dominates our society. In certain Christian circles a faith mission or 'to live by faith' implies a claim to be looking to God alone for daily needs. Though such an expression has no real Biblical justification and can be very uncharitable towards some other Christian workers, it is a tacit recognition of the difficulty of refusing to conform to the present world system. It is almost always easier to separate oneself from what one deems to be incorrect churchmanship than to abandon the mutual benefit system of the world. The call reflects the position in 13.16, and is addressed to those who by continued conformity risk their souls; coming out would preserve their souls even though it risked their bodies.

We are reminded of Psa. 137.7–9 by v. 6. One of the achievements of Babylon is to hide from us the worst evils it commits. Even the Press watch-dog is apt to deal with evil facts as the cinema does with the heroine lost in the African jungle. She may emerge in rags, but she looks as though she had just left the beauty parlour. Somehow the real evil in evil is normally eliminated before it reaches us in print and picture. On the other hand we have 'selective condemnation', where we see only those evils that are committed by those outside our political views and ideologies. The call of vs. 4–8 reminds us that evil when seen by heaven is blacker. 'To know all is to forgive all' is not one of God's maxims!

Thought: Lot was not the only righteous man that has lived in Sodom.

Revelation 18.9-19 The Lament over Babylon

There is no more honourable call open to man than to be king, as the term was and should be understood, for the king should make God's rule real to his subjects. But few have been the kings who realized their high calling and so have gone down in history as 'the Good'. By most it was understood not as a call to serve but to be served, cf. Mark 10.42–44. For them Babylon was the means by which they received the baubles their office brought them; hence their lamentation (10).

The real losers are the merchants. We should read through their list carefully, weighing each item and asking ourselves how neces-

80

sary they are (12,13). Few of the goods will pass the scrutiny of eternity, though some may make life easier and more pleasant. The list ends with 'slaves'. It does not matter whether we take 'human souls' as a qualification (so RSV), or render 'and the lives of men' (NEB). Commerce is bitterly condemned here and in the O.T., because normally it pays so little attention to the good of those involved in it. Today it is often merely a question whether human labour or machines are cheaper. This is not a condemnation of commerce, but of commerce as it has been twisted by the world. It is clear that God so made the world that no individual or country can be completely autonomous. For modern life even giants like the USA and Russia are not completely self-supporting. Perhaps the most telling condemnation of it is 1 Kings 10.22, with which compare 1 Kings 10.16–21,27.

The selfishness of the whole business is seen in the fact that kings, merchants and sailors alike think merely of what they have lost. There is no sign of sympathy with those who have perished, not even with those with whom they had personal business links. We need to put the person of our Lord against this background and then reread Matt. 6.25–34. Teaching, which seems idealistic and even impossible, becomes possible in the light of Christ and practical in the light of Babylon's end.

Thought: Seek the things that are above where Christ is.

Revelation 18.20-24   The Doom of Babylon

It is very strange that the RSV should have taken v. 20 as the close of the mariners' lament. If it were so, their sudden recognition of the role of heaven, and the justification of those who had lost their lives in or through Babylon would run counter to the whole trend of the chapter. Rather, v. 20 would seem to be John's own comment, showing his deep satisfaction. The NEB seems to be correct in rendering, 'for in the judgement against her He has vindicated your cause!' Whether we think of Babylon as a place or a system, as religious or commercial, there seems no reason why its judgement should anticipate the general judgement. It could have been swept away in the dust caused by the Return, cf. Dan. 2.34 f. But even under the conditions of this age it had to be shown that in the end Lowell's lines do not apply:

> 'Truth for ever on the scaffold,
> Wrong for ever on the throne.'

81

There follows the symbolic sign of the doom of Babylon (21), cf. Jer. **51**.63 f. It should be noted that we are not told exactly how Babylon the harlot and the city perish. The foretelling of Scripture is to enable us to recognize God's hand, when He brings His purpose to pass, not to enable us to flaunt our knowledge by being able to tell people exactly how things are to come about.

Just as the destruction of the harlot is not something sudden like a bolt out of the blue, but is being foreshadowed by much that has happened during the past two centuries, so too, just at the time when international commerce seems to have reached its height, there are growing signs of its breaking down.

The harlot offers man second-rate religion, the outward appearance without the inner reality. International commerce draws the world closer together, not to create true brotherhood, but to make exploitation easier. The true believer, by true fellowship with his Lord and true brotherhood with his fellow, shows up the hollowness of Babylon. That is why he is hated and persecuted.

Thought: The love of money is a root of all manner of evil.

Revelation 19.1-5 Joy in Heaven

We are accustomed to think of joy in heaven over a sinner that repents. Here it is ultimately over those who will never be able to repent. This may seem frightful, until we remember that it is over those who made it so hard for others to believe, those who fought to the last against the truth, those who were the incarnation of Satan's hatred even as the Church is of Christ's love. In addition, Christ in His judgement of the great white throne can discriminate between those who had sold themselves to the Satanic powers for gain and power, and those deluded ones who were swept along by the current of the age.

The NEB does well to render 'the roar of a vast throng' (1); it reverberates like peals of thunder, cf. v. 6. 'The smoke from her' (3); for mortal minds it is as difficult to conceive of perfect sinless bliss as of utter, inexorably just condemnation. Therefore both are described in purely symbolic language, which should always be treated as such. The best chapter to study the symbolic language of judgement is probably Isa. **34**. In vs. 1–4 we have universal judgement involving even the heavenly bodies (but are they rulers?); the earth is strewn with corpses and the mountains flow with blood. In v. 5 the general judgement is particularized by Edom, and in vs. 6,7 we have the soil manured with fat and blood. In vs. 8–10 we have it as active volcanic waste—note v. 10b—but in vs. 11–17 it is inhabited by animals, real and mythological, that do not live among pitch and brimstone. From this we should grasp that we do not have any unitary picture of judgement; we are allowed to judge of its reality by the juxtaposition of mutually incompatible pictures which give some idea of the awefulness of God's judgement. The picture of smoke continually rising (**19.3**, cf. **18.**18; Isa. **34.**10) is taken from Gen. **19.**28, thus linking the destruction of Babylon with that of Sodom and Gomorrah.

Thought: It is a fearful thing to fall into the hands of the living God.

Revelation 19.6-10   The Marriage of the Lamb

The concept of Israel as the wife of Jehovah is at least as old as *Hosea*, and figures prominently in *Jeremiah* and *Ezekiel* as well as the second half of *Isaiah*. The thought behind it is partly that of God's love, partly of His covenant loyalty, partly that Israel by representing Jehovah 'completes' Him upon earth. The concept was then taken over by the Church, especially as Christ = Messiah = King, and a king must have a people. When that people was thought of as expressing His character, the picture of the vine and branches was used (John **15.**1–8), the fruit being the fruit of the Spirit (Gal. **5.**22 f.). When the Church is looked on as serving and representing Christ, it is called His body. When the fellowship between the Church and its Saviour is stressed, then it is His wife (Eph. **5.**21–33; this passage shows that there is no contradiction between the pictures of body and wife). Since engagement in Israel was equivalent to marraige, the Church can be called the wife of Christ now, but the fullness awaits the victory of Christ through the Church.

One of the loveliest pictures in the N.T. has been obscured in the AV(KJV); 'the fine linen is the righteous deeds of the saints' (8). The picture evoked is of a great loom in heaven; every righteous deed, i.e. every act produced by our being accounted righteous in Christ, is carried up to the angel weaver, who incorporates it in the material of the wedding dress, designed to bring glory to the Bridegroom, not the bride.

Needless discussion has raged around 'Blessed are those who are invited' (9), cf. the Ten Virgins (Matt. **25.**1–13). By its nature, symbolism is never the complete expression of truth. Terms like body and wife refer to the Church corporate, local or universal, and not to the individual. Hence in symbolic language we can have the wedding feast and yet those who compose the wife, the conquerors, invited to it.

'For testimony to Jesus is the spirit that inspires prophets' (10, NEB, margin) seems to give the meaning best. The angel refused to let his testimony bring him worship, i.e. honour. Wherever the prophet brings honour to himself instead of Jesus, his message is not from God. The interpreter of prophecy who draws attention to others than Jesus, or to himself by his cleverness, has lost his way.

Thought: At the name of Jesus every knee shall bow.

Revelation 19.11-21   The Victorious Word of God

The title, Word of God, which was hinted at in 1.16 and given in John 1.1, comes victoriously (13). Jesus Christ has been the perfect expression and performer of God's will from beginning to end. The only weapon mentioned is His sword (21), which is His words; a similar concept is found in 2 Thess. 2.8. If there is war at all in this passage, it is spiritual and not physical. In fact it is questionable whether there is war at all. How can any stand against the unveiled glory of Christ?

'A white horse' (11): the sign of the conqueror, cf. 6.2. 'Faithful and True', i.e. Trustworthy and Dependable. 'Like a flame of fire' (12), cf. 1.14. 'Many diadems', in contrast to the seven (12.3) and ten (13.1); all authority is Christ's. The name known only to Himself (12) probably refers to the very widely spread superstition in antiquity that knowledge of a man's or god's name can give power over him; none can control the Lord, and there is no formula of words that can force Him to do our bidding. 'Dipped in blood' (13): not 'sprinkled with' as in the margin. Sprinkling was for cleansing from sin; here it is His own blood and replaces 'as though He had been slain' in the description of the Lamb (5.6). 'The armies of heaven' (14): this is a victory parade. 'Wine press' (15): see notes on 14.19. 'His thigh' (16): this probably means His girdle.

The call of the angel (17) does not invalidate the earlier remark about the absence of fighting. The symbolism of war is carried on throughout. The enemies of Christ are destroyed that they may await the general resurrection. If the beast and the false prophet are treated differently, it is because they are systems and not merely persons, cf. also 20.13, where death and Hades are also so treated. This should warn us against dogmatism in our understanding of 'the lake of fire' (20). The picture is symbolic, but that does not entitle us to strip it of meaning. Symbolism always expresses less than the whole truth. The modern reaction against the crudities of the mediaeval concept of hell should merely be a challenge to us to envisage something worse and more tragic for those who find their eternal destiny there.

Revelation 20.1-6 The Millennium

There is always a strong temptation for the theologian to try to avoid the obvious teaching of symbolism, if it does not fit in with his theories. Now that so much more is known of Talmudic and Inter-Testamental Jewish writings, it is beyond dispute that John is referring to the 'days of the Messiah', the period which links this age with the world to come. Any other interpretation would force on the prophecy a meaning its first hearers could not have understood.

Two interpretations seem compatible with this. One claims that the triumph of Christ in 19.11-21 is purely spiritual and that it is followed by a long period of the triumphant Church bringing blessing to the world before the final revolt and the return of Christ in judgement. The fact that Augustine, and after him most in the mediaeval Church, thought that they had already entered the Millennium does not invalidate this interpretation. The other is that 19.11-21 shows the return of Christ, and that the Millennium follows it, the world being in some way under the personal rule of Christ. This view has more difficulties in it than its supporters often realize, but it certainly fits the evidence of the N.T. better. Rightly understood the two views are not so far apart as is often thought. Both should see Christ's triumph through the Church, and both should look to the future for the open revelation of it.

The purpose of the long history of God's dealings with men is to make them realize that only through complete trust in and obedience to God can there be true blessing. The final lesson that men have to learn is that the root of the trouble is *in* them and not outside; so Satan, having been defeated, is for the time being rendered incapable of doing his work.

While there is not much about 'the first resurrection' (5) in the N.T., it is indubitably there. It is implied in Luke 14.14 and probably in 1 Cor. 15.23; it is stated in 1 Thess. 4.16 and probably in the Greek of Phil. 3.11. Since all resurrection is the outcome of Christ's, the N.T. avoids giving the impression that the earlier resurrection of the conquerors is in any way a result of their own merits. The nature of the 'judgement' (4) is not specified, but there is no indication that it has anything to do with the dead. There is, however, no suggestion of sinlessness during the Millennium.

Revelation 20.7-15 The Final Judgement

Organized evil and opposition to God need a leader, and so Satan is released to show that essentially man has not changed. Gog and Magog, cf. Ezek. 38.2,3, seem to represent all those peoples who have been on the fringe of civilization and therefore only marginally involved with the beast. The use of 'camp' (9) may be an indication that even the Millennium is not the final goal of the Church, cf. Heb. 11.10; Rev. 21.2, though Phillip's translation 'the army of the saints defending the beloved city' is worthy of consideration. It is striking how little is told us of the Millennium.

The One who sits on the 'great white throne' (11) is presumably Jesus Christ, cf. John 5.22,27. The throne represents rule, and white purity. Faced by it even material creation cannot abide it; 21.1 makes clear, however, that there is no thought of the abolition of the world. The 'books' (12), cf. Dan. 7.10, are doubtless the record of human history, though we should hesitate to take them literally. We should remember that this is genuine judgement, not merely a parade for judgement, though there are those who appear only to hear the sentence, cf. John 3.18. The books give evidence of the man's life and character, but the verdict is based on 'the book of life'; in other words, acquittal is by grace. The idea that the book of life is opened merely to show that a man's name is not there is almost blasphemous. We may be certain that the hardened Jew (Rom. 11.25), the Gentile who has never heard, and all those who have seen and heard only perversions of the gospel, will be treated accordingly. We can accept without hesitation that the Judge, who was the sin offering for all men, will say to some, 'Your life shows that if you had heard, or heard properly, you would have believed.' We may imagine some of them who had never heard falling at His feet in adoration, as they recognize the One they had always longed for. We are not entitled to think that Satan will have the satisfaction of drawing the bulk of mankind with him to hell. That some will be lost we know; our estimate of how many will be saved is likely to depend on our estimate of the power and love of God.

'The second death' (14): it might be better, if we were to use this term rather than hell. Death is that which makes it impossible for man to accomplish his dreams and God's will. As he stands before the great white throne he knows what he is and what he has missed, but there remains no hope of ever changing or achieving.

Questions for further study and discussion on Revelation chs. 18–20
1. What is meant by Babylon?
2. Note the emphasis on wealth and luxury in ch. 18. What does the N.T. have to say concerning riches and those who have them?
3. Note those portions in *Revelation* which give praise to God and Christ. For what specific reasons is praise given?
4. Bearing in mind 19.8 show from 1 John and Matt. 25 that the thought of the coming of Christ is meant to spur us on to greater holiness of life.
5. 'Persecution' and 'expansion' are two key words in Church history. Illustrate this from *Acts* and later Church history.
6. What does the Bible teach about Satan?
7. Who will be judged, and on what basis?

Revelation 21.1-8   God with Man

'A new heaven' (1): this is the same word as in 20.11; it is the sky and not God's home that is meant. The word for new in Greek implies that there is some link with the old, just as there is between our resurrection bodies and those that now are. The 'new Jerusalem' is the wife of the Lamb (9), i.e. the glorified Church. Contrary to popular opinion the age to come does not see the abolition of this creation in favour of heaven—that is a legacy of Greek thought with its despising of the material—but its transformation through its being linked with heaven by the glorified Church. 'With men' (3): not the Church but the new nations (24). It is likely that we should translate v. 3 as 'God-with-them shall Himself be their God' (NEB, margin), i.e. we have finally the complete fulfilment of the promise of Isa. 7.14.

In this section of *Revelation* we do not merely have a picture of the future, for the Bible is never interested in the future merely as future, but in its bearing on our lives in the present. So repeatedly there is a message addressed to the reader, e.g. vs. 5–8. 'Trustworthy and true' (5): the same as the name in 19.11—as the speaker so His words. 'It is done' (6): what John had seen was not to find its fulfilment until many centuries had rolled by, but since God is the Creator and Sustainer from beginning to end, His decree would bring the vision to certain fruition.

Those who are finally to enjoy these things must be like Christ (1 John 3.2) and be God's sons because they have been transformed into the image of the Son of God. Exclusion is due to lack of Christlikeness. The sins mentioned fall into three categories. Liars (cf. 14.5), cowards, faithless persons (i.e. those who having no faith in God cannot be trusted) are those who fear their fellow men rather than God, and who place the judgement of man above that of God. The murderers and fornicators destroy the lives of men that are and of the children that have not yet been conceived. Then there are the idolaters, those who would make God in their own image, and the sorcerers, those who seek to twist God round their own will by magic of all kinds; such men are polluted, for they have no interest in the cleansing that only God can offer.

Thought: You can be made new!

Revelation 21.9-21   The New Jerusalem

It has already been pointed out that we are dealing with the glorified Church (9). If the gates have the names of 'the twelve tribes' (12), and the foundations those of 'the twelve apostles' (14), it means that the true Israel and the victorious Church, whose essential unity of being has been assumed throughout the book, have now coalesced, though we are not told how. Those who speak of a heavenly calling for the Church and an earthly one for the Jew are correct only on a short-term view.

'Twelve thousand stadia' are about 1500 miles. A perfect cube (16) of such dimensions makes no practical sense, especially if it has a wall only '144 cubits' (17), i.e. 216 feet, high. We can, however, interpret it in terms of Ezek. 40.2 and see a pyramid-shaped mountain. But instead of there being a relatively small temple on the summit, the city, which received only passing notice in Ezek. 48.30–35 (note the twelve gates), has now filled the mountain, cf. also Dan. 2.35; Isa. 11.9. The measurements are, of course, as symbolic as the city itself. Spurgeon in one of his lectures made fun of the literalist by calculating the size of the oyster needed to produce 'a pearl' (21) large enough to form a city gate, and speculated on the kind of sea needed to grow such an oyster. Those used to abstract or poetic thought can be satisfied with 'having the glory of God' (11), but for the more primitive or childlike mind this has to be expressed in material terms.

Eight of the precious stones in vs. 19 f. are found in the standard Greek translation of Exod. 28.17–20, though not in this order. It is a safe guess then that they are meant to be the twelve stones of the breastplate of judgement, the Greek version available to John using other names in the missing positions. If this is so, any symbolic meaning in the stones must be sought in their O.T. significance. The walls are founded on judgement, but also, on the love and thought of God, for the breastplate was worn over Aaron's heart. Yet the values of the city are not those of this world, for gold, for which many men will sell their souls, is of no more value than to be used as a paving material to be trodden underfoot.

Revelation 21.22—22.5   I Saw No Temple There

We think of a temple normally as a place where men worship God. In fact, both with the Tabernacle and the Temple the real purpose was to separate the worshippers from God. Into the Holy of Holies with its cherub throne for God, only the High Priest could come one day in the year; only priests were allowed in the Holy Place, and that when they were carrying out their duties. Into the court of the Tabernacle and the inner court of the Temple the ceremonially clean Israelite man could enter only as he brought his sacrifices. In the Tabernacle court there was no room for the woman or the man without a sacrifice. In the Temple John had known, the Court of the Israelite, the Courts of the Women and of the Gentiles had decreasing stages of sanctity, but in the strictest sense they were not part of the sanctuary. The reason for the separation was to keep apart Divine holiness and human sin. Already Jeremiah foresaw the day when Jerusalem, not the Ark, would 'be called the throne of the Lord' (Jer. 3.17). Now the vision is fulfilled. Sin has gone, so the dividing walls have, too (22).

'Night shall be no more' (5,25): physical conditions under the conditions of eternity are unknowable. Once again we have symbolism, where night and darkness represent evil, sin and absence of God, cf. John 1.5; 1 John 1.5, even as the sea in 21.1 is once again lawlessness.

One of the great weaknesses of traditional theology is that it tends to overlook in practice the universality of atonement and makes the Church the only sphere of salvation. Yet we have 'the nations . . . and the kings of the earth' (24) in addition to the city, i.e. the Church. Among them there is not perfection, for unlike the Church they need 'healing' (2) even in eternity.

We are given three aspects of the eternal state. 'His servants', literally slaves, 'shall worship Him' (3): neither the Christian's title nor occupation, cf. Rom. **12.**1, has changed, only the degree of perfection. 'They shall see His face' (4): though we now see in a mirror dimly (1 Cor. **13.**12), the fellowship implied has already begun. 'His name shall be on their foreheads': this awaits Christ's coming (1 John **3.**2), but the process of transformation is already going on (2 Cor. **3.**18), cf. **14.**1.

Thought: The life of eternity begins down here.

Revelation 22.6-15   I Come Quickly!

For v. 6, cf. **19.**11; **21.**5. We meet a crux in interpretation in vs. 6,7; '. . . what must soon take place . . . I am coming soon', cf. **3.**11; **22.**20. It is increasingly being claimed that the apostles were mistaken about our Lord's teaching on His return, or even that they projected their own ideas into His teaching. Hence, it is suggested, we need not take the Second Advent teaching of the N.T. seriously. The one answer we may not give is that the time-measure used is God's. The answer lies in another direction. If the exposition has achieved its purpose, it will have made clear the timelessness of so much in *Revelation,* so that men were justified in thinking that its prophecies were going into effect in their day. It is not important when Christ comes but that He comes, and that there has never been a time since the destruction of Jerusalem when He could not have come. It is our attitude to the Coming that matters, cf. 2 Tim. **4.**8, and we are meant to be on the watch.

'I fell down to worship' (8), cf. **19.**10: the Greek word is used of any act of profound respect, especially prostration, to high-ranking persons as well as gods. Hence it is used frequently in the N.T. in settings where 'worship' is misleading. John, the Jew, could never have thought of worshipping an angel. It is his extreme respect that is being rejected. Those entrusted with the Word are apt to expect undue honour from men, cf. John **5.**43 f.

In v. 11 we have neither indifference to men's salvation, nor a suggestion that there is no hope for those mentioned. The man who has taken in the warnings of 'this book' (10) and has gone his way unchanged has little hope of changing. While we may not exclude hope so long as there is life; we should have little for the man who has repeatedly heard and repeatedly rejected. Theoretically 'the gates' should come before 'the tree of life' (14), but since both are pictures of Christ, it represents the normal order. He who practises falsehood will come to love it (15). 'The dogs': cf. Matt **7.**6;

Phil. **3.2**, an epithet often applied by the Jews to the heathen. It is doubtful whether 'depraved' (Phillips) is an adequate rendering; rather the person without a sense of values or morals is intended— the dog was the scavenger of the ancient city.

Revelation 22.16-21 Come, Lord Jesus!

For 'the root and the offspring of David' (16), cf. **5.5**. While we are accustomed to think of the O.T. as being summed up in Jesus Christ, we must never forget that it is also the unfolding of His will. 'The bright morning star': two lines of thought converge here. He is the star of Num. **24.17**, proclaimed by the star of Matt. **2.2**. He is also the abiding hope as the night grows long, proclaiming that dawn cannot be far off.

It is normal to take 'Come' (17) as a call to Christ, as in v. 20. In the context, however, it is more likely to be the appeal to those outside. Day has not yet come, so while the day star is yet to be seen, the continued appeal goes out.

For anyone to add to or subtract from the Scriptures is a spiritual hardihood for which a man will have to give his answer in the judgement. But that is not the point of vs. 18,19, which refer only to *Revelation*. In looking at the world around us it is easy for one with a reputation as a prophetic expert to convince himself that he is witnessing the fulfilment of the prophecy and so quietly to twist it slightly to prove his thesis. On the other hand, passages that do not suit it can be quietly ignored. It is this way of treating prophecy that has brought it into such disrepute.

For those who live where man has not befouled the world, it can be very beautiful. Man has created much which must arouse our admiration and regard in art, music, architecture and literature, though part of his handiwork suggests hell rather than heaven for its place of origin. Married love and the family are such that God is willing to use their language to express His relationship to His people. But over the best there lies the shadow of death, reminding us that sin has left its mark on all. Once the light of the Coming falls on the scene around us, it is like the traditional transformation scene in the pantomime, where all relationships are changed. *Revelation* has showed us that beauty and ease for the Christian are merely the calm at the centre of the cyclone, while the attractiveness of the world hides the corruption beneath. So the heart cries yearningly, 'Come, Lord Jesus!' Till He does, it remains true:

Yea, thro' life, death, thro' sorrow and thro' sinning
He shall suffice me, for He hath sufficed:
Christ is the end, for Christ was the beginning,
Christ the beginning, for the end is Christ.

Questions for further study and discussion on Revelation chs. 21,22

1. What does the N.T. teach about heaven?
2. What do we learn from 22.11a and Rom. 1.18–32 about (*i*) God and (*ii*) man?
3. What can be said with certainty about the Second Coming?
4. How is the sovereignty of God in the world depicted in *Revelation?*
5. For what reasons was the *Revelation* written? Are these relevant today?
6. In what sense can more that one interpretation of *Revelation* be valid?